EACL Workshop on Language Technology and Resources for Cultural Heritage, Social Sciences, Humanities, and Education 2009

(LaTeCH-SHELT&R 2009)

Held in Conjunction with EACL 2009

Athens, Greece
30 March 2009

ISBN: 978-1-61738-560-5

Printed from e-media with permission by:

Curran Associates, Inc.
57 Morehouse Lane
Red Hook, NY 12571

Some format issues inherent in the e-media version may also appear in this print version.

Printed by Curran Associates, Inc. (2010)

For permission requests, please contact the Association for Computational Linguistics at the address below.

Association for Computational Linguistics
209 N. Eighth Street
Stroudsburg, Pennsylvania 18360

Phone: 1-570-476-8006
Fax: 1-570-476-0860

acl@aclweb.org

Additional copies of this publication are available from:

Curran Associates, Inc.
57 Morehouse Lane
Red Hook, NY 12571 USA
Phone: 845-758-0400
Fax: 845-758-2634
Email: curran@proceedings.com
Web: www.proceedings.com

Preface

The LaTeCH–SHELT&R workshop aims to present in one forum two strands of research in language technology, which we believe have many common concerns, but also complementary viewpoints.

Museums, archives, and libraries around the world maintain large collections of cultural heritage objects, such as archaeological artefacts, sound recordings, historical manuscripts, or preserved animal specimens. Large scale digitization projects are currently underway to make these collections more accessible to the public and to research. The natural next step after digitization is the development of powerful tools to search, link, enrich, and mine the digitized data. Language technology has an important role to play in this endeavor, even for collections which are primarily non-textual, since text is the pervasive medium used for metadata. Two previous LaTeCH (*Language Technology for Cultural Heritage*) workshops (at ACL 2007 in Prague and LREC 2008 in Marrakech) have shown that there is an interest among language technology researchers in providing intelligent infrastructure and tools for working with cultural heritage data.

Similarly, in research in the Social Sciences, Humanities and Education (SHE), text – and speech, i.e., *language* – are central as both primary and secondary research data sources. In today's world, the normal mode of access to text, speech, images and video is in digital form. Modern material is born digital, and, as already mentioned, older material is being digitized on a vast scale in cultural heritage and digital library projects. Language technology and language resources has an equally important role to play here, as in the cultural heritage area, and for more or less the same purposes. A clear sign of this is the newly launched European research infrastructure initiative CLARIN, which addresses exactly the use of language technology and language resources as research infrastructure in the humanities and social sciences. Against this background, it now seems natural to add a component to the workshop reflecting this development: SHELT&R (*Language Technology and Resources infrastructure for text-based research in the Social Sciences, Humanities and Education*).

The CH and SHE domains are not mere passive consumers of ready-made language technology solutions. Rather, they make up interesting and challenging testbeds, where the robustness and the generality of existing language technology are subjected to the acid test of messy and multilingual reality, more so than in many other application areas, since they have to deal with, *inter alia*, historical, non-standardized language varieties in addition to a number of modern standard languages. Our workshop thus aims to foster interaction between researchers working on all aspects of language technology applied to the CH and SHE domains, and experts from institutions who are testing deployed technologies and formulating improved use cases.

The papers accepted for the LaTeCH–SHELT&R workshop after a thorough peer-review process give a good sense of the current breadth of this exciting and expanding area. We are happy that our keynote speakers, Dr. Martin Doerr and Dr. Tamás Váradi, agreed to join us and deliver excellent topics for a complete workshop program. We would like to thank all authors who submitted papers for the hard work that went into their submissions. We are also extremely grateful to the members of the programme committee for providing thorough reviews and multi-faceted input.

Some of the workshop costs were covered from a project grant awarded to Lars Borin by the Swedish Research Council (VR Dnr 2007-7430: *Safeguarding the future of Språkbanken*), which is hereby gratefully acknowledged.

Lars Borin • *Piroska Lendvai*

LaTeCH – SHELT&R 2009

Workshop Chairs:

Lars Borin, University of Gothenburg (Sweden)
Piroska Lendvai, Tilburg University (The Netherlands)

Organizing Committe:

Piroska Lendvai (Co-chair), Tilburg University (The Netherlands)
Lars Borin (Co-chair), University of Gothenburg (Sweden)
Antal van den Bosch, Tilburg University (The Netherlands)
Martin Reynaert, Tilburg University (The Netherlands)
Caroline Sporleder, Saarland University (Germany)

Program Committee Members:

Ion Androutsopoulos, Athens University of Economics and Business (Greece)
Timothy Baldwin, University of Melbourne (Australia)
David Bamman, Perseus (USA)
Lars Borin, University of Gothenburg (Sweden)
Antal van den Bosch, Tilburg University (The Netherlands)
Andrea Bozzi, ILC-CNR, Pisa (Italy)
Paul Buitelaar, DERI Galway (Ireland)
Kate Byrne, University of Edinburgh (UK)
Claire Cardie, Cornell University (USA)
Paul Clough, Sheffield University (UK)
Milena P. Dobreva, CDLR, University of Strathclyde (UK)
Mick O'Donnell, Universidad Autonoma de Madrid (Spain)
Claire Grover, University of Edinburgh (UK)
Ben Hachey, University of Edinburgh (UK)
Erhard Hinrichs, Tübingen University (Germany)
Graeme Hirst, University of Toronto (Canada)
Christer Johansson, University of Bergen (Norway)
Jaap Kamps, University of Amsterdam (The Netherlands)
Dimitrios Kokkinakis, University of Gothenburg (Sweden)
Stasinos Konstantopoulos, NCSR Demokritos (Greece)
Piroska Lendvai, Tilburg University (The Netherlands)
Christina Lioma, University of Leuven (Belgium)
Anke Lüdeling, Humboldt University (Germany)
Veronique Malaisé, Free University of Amsterdam (The Netherlands)
Steven van der Mije, Trezorix (The Netherlands)
John Nerbonne, Rijksuniversiteit Groningen (The Netherlands)
Marco Pennacchiotti, Saarland University/Yahoo! Research (Germany)
Georg Rehm, vionto GmbH, Berlin (Germany)
Martin Reynaert, Tilburg University (The Netherlands)
Michael Rosner, University of Malta (Malta)
Caroline Sporleder, Saarland University (Germany)
Tamás Váradi, Hungarian Academy of Sciences (Hungary)
Andreas Witt, Tübingen University (Germany)
Svitlana Zinger, Eindhoven University of Technology (The Netherlands)

Table of Contents

Conference Program

Monday, March 30, 2009

9:00–9.15 Opening

9:15–10:15 Invited Talk by Martin Doerr

10:15–10:30 Moderated discussion

10:30–11:00 Coffee break

11:00–11:30 *Content Analysis of Museum Documentation in a Transdisciplinary Perspective*
Guenther Goerz and Martin Scholz

11:30–12:00 *An Intelligent Authoring Environment for Abstract Semantic Representations of Cultural Object Descriptions*
Stasinos Konstantopoulos, Vangelis Karkaletsis and Dimitris Bilidas

12:00–12:20 *Multiple Sequence Alignments in Linguistics*
Jelena Prokić, Martijn Wieling and John Nerbonne

12:20–12:45 *Evaluating the Pairwise String Alignment of Pronunciations*
Martijn Wieling, Jelena Prokić and John Nerbonne

12:45–14:00 Lunch

14:00–15:00 Invited talk by Tamás Váradi

15:00–15:20 *A Web-Enabled and Speech-Enhanced Parallel Corpus of Greek-Bulgarian Cultural Texts*
Voula Giouli, Nikos Glaros, Kiril Simov and Petya Osenova

15:20–15:40 *The Development of the "Index Thomisticus" Treebank Valency Lexicon*
Barbara McGillivray and Marco Passarotti

15:40–16:00 *Applying NLP Technologies to the Collection and Enrichment of Language Data on the Web to Aid Linguistic Research*
Fei Xia and William Lewis

16:00–16:30 Coffee break

Monday, March 30, 2009 (continued)

16:30–16:55 *Instance-Driven Discovery of Ontological Relation Labels*
Marieke van Erp, Antal van den Bosch, Sander Wubben and Steve Hunt

16:55–17:20 *The Role of Metadata in the Longevity of Cultural Heritage Resources*
Milena Dobreva and Nikola Ikonomov

17:25–18:00 Moderated discussion; closing

Content Analysis of Museum Documentation with a Transdisciplinary Perspective

Günther Goerz, Martin Scholz
University of Erlangen-Nuremberg, Computer Science Department (8)
Erlangen, Germany
goerz@informatik.uni-erlangen.de

Abstract

In many cases, museum documentation consists of semi-structured data records with free text fields, which usually refer to contents of other fields, in the same data record, as well as in others. Most of these references comprise of person and place names, as well as time specifications. It is, therefore, important to recognize those in the first place. We report on techniques and results of partial parsing in an ongoing project, using a large database on German goldsmith art. The texts are encoded according to the TEI guidelines and expanded by structured descriptions of named entities and time specifications. These are building blocks for event descriptions, at which the next step is aiming. The identification of named entities allows the data to be linked with various resources within the domain of cultural heritage and beyond. For the latter case, we refer to a biological database and present a solution in a transdisciplinary perspective by means of the CIDOC Conceptual Reference Model (CRM).

1 Specific Goals of Content Analysis

When we speak of museum documentation, we address a wide variety of document types. First of all, there are acquisition and inventory lists or index cards, which contain more or less detailed records of museum objects. Often these are accompanied by photographs, restoration records, and further archival records. If curators prepare exhibitions, usually they provide catalogs by compiling data from sources, such as those just mentioned, and by contributing short articles on the exhibits. Last but not least there are scholarly monographs on museum objects.

With the introduction of information technology in museums and cultural heritage institutions, such records have been stored in (relational) database systems and content management systems. At the beginning — with the exception of bibliographic records — there were no metadata standards at all in the museum world. Since the 1990s, many metadata schemata have been proposed for the field of cultural heritage, some with very detailed classification features for specific object types[1]. There is still an active discussion about metadata schemata and their standardisation, as can be seen with recent proposals for CDWA Lite, museumdat and their combination (Stein and Coburn, 2008).

Today, access to museum documentation via the World Wide Web has become a matter of course, in particular, if the documentation has been the result of publicly funded research projects. Naturally, printed editions are still a very important medium of publication. However, in many cases the data are too voluminous, which means only abridged versions are published in print, while the full data are available only in digital form. Web access allows many means to retrieve and print the data, with very little cost involved. Using controlled language defined in terminologies and formal ontologies, different forms of "intelligent search" come within reach as well as interactive evaluation and visualisation methods. But it is not only access to the data alone; interactivity opens up possibilites for Wiki-style annotation and scholarly communication, as well as forums for the general public. Furthermore, the technology provides methods to link the data with other resources, e.g. authority files containing biographical or geographical data.

[1] cf. Getty Foundation's Metadata Crosswalk http://www.getty.edu/research/conducting_research/standards/intrometadata/crosswalks.html ;visited 03.12.2008.

Proceedings of the EACL 2009 Workshop on Language Technology and Resources for Cultural Heritage, Social Sciences, Humanities, and Education –LaTeCH – SHELT&R 2009, pages 1–9,
Athens, Greece, 30 March 2009.

A common situation in museum documentation is characterized by the fact that it is centered around museum objects, i.e. there is a database system or content management system, which contains structured descriptions of museum objects and further information about their creators, provenance, use, and so forth, according to given descriptive and administrative metadata schemata. Besides fields in such data records enforcing (more or less strictly defined) data types, e.g. for inventory numbers, there are free text fields which contain important background information about persons, objects, materials, stylistic festures, etc. without any further tagging. Basically, the free text fields are open for any kind of information which cannot be expressed in the strictly defined parts of the schema. Therefore, overall, the given data records at best provide a semi-structured representation.

The free text fields and their relations to other fields, in particular, indicate a clear need for content analysis. Firstly, named entitities must be identified, in particular person and geographic place names. For instance, there may be a data field for the creator of a work of art and another one for the place where this work was created, additionally one or more free text fields which talk about the artist's family relations, when he came to the mentioned place and how long he stayed there, etc. As this example indicates, at least a second type of linguistic expressions, time specifications in a variety of forms, ought to be recognized. In the future, we would like to identify event descriptions and how they are related among each other, for which the recognition of named entitites and time specifications is a first step.

In the following sections we describe our approach to address these problems. The next section outlines characteristic features of the data with a reflection on their typicality. Section three is the central technical part presenting the shallow text analysis techniques we use — word class tagging, recognition of temporal specifications, place and person names — and the utilization of name authorities for lexical and semantic enrichment. In the fourth section we show how the results achieved so far can be used to construct event-based shallow semantic representations related to the CIDOC CRM. Furthermore, the CRM is also the key to transdisciplinary approaches in museum documentation as outlined in the final section with an example between biology and cultural history.

2 Characteristics of the Data

We are working[2] with data which resulted from a project on goldsmith art in Nuremberg, executed at the German National Museum, providing descriptions of more than 6700 objects, 2290 artists, many locations, etc. Furthermore, with the museum's content management system we can access many more data records on sculptures and paintings — with a particular emphasis on the work of Albrecht Dürer — up to 1800. The latter corpora were accessed primarily to verify the general usefulness of the approach that will be presented in the following sections.

For many projects in the field of cultural heritage in Germany, a condition for public funding has been to use the MIDAS[3] data schema (Heusinger, 1989) in combination with a specific database implementation (HiDA). MIDAS defines a framework of record types with appropriate properties for terms (thesauri), time, place, artists, other persons and organizations, objects, content and signs, events, sources, and administrative data. The goal of MIDAS was to establish a de facto standard based on the current documentation practice in museums. Depending on what is to be documented, the appropriate record types can be selected. HiDA is a data administration system, which provides a graphical user interface for data input, editing, and search; it stores the records not in a database system, but in a system of files, one for each type, in a proprietary format. For this reason and problems in handling the user interface, many HiDA-encoded data are now being converted to an XML representation. For the free texts, we decided to follow the encoding rules of the Text Encoding Initiative (TEI) (Ide and Veronis, 1995)[4] for text bodies.

The actual encoding of the XML-transformed data sets is still very close to HiDA as far as the "classes" and properties are concerned. Currently, the data are in the process of being transformed to the emerging museumdat/CDWA Lite

[2]Research project "WissKI — Wissenschaftliche KommunikationsInfrastruktur"; funding provided by the German Research Council (DFG)

[3]Acronym for "Marburger Informations-, Dokumentations- und Administrations-System", not to be confused with the MIDAS heritage standard in the UK.

[4]Website: `http://www.tei-c.org/index.xml`; visited 15.12.2008

standard (Stein and Coburn, 2008)[5], which in turn is compatible with CIDOC's Conceptual Reference Model (Doerr, 2003)[6]. The CRM is the formal reference ontology, which defines the conceptual background for the semantic representations resulting from content analysis. We refer to the CRM as a formally defined reference ontology because with the "Erlangen CRM"[7] we provided is a description logic version of the latest standard (ISO 21127:2009), implemented in OWL-DL (Goerz et al., 2008).

As for the content of the free text fields, the texts contain well-formed sentences in the linguistic sense, although in some cases, one can find elliptic formulations in telegraphic style. In most cases, the texts refer to defined data record fields (persons, creatorship, object properties, bibliographic data), providing additional information, for which there is no other place in the schema. A great deal of the texts talk about family and other relations between persons, about creatorship, techniques, actions of the mentioned persons other than the creation of the artwork, and the general cultural context. As in early modern German there is a great orthographic variation even in writing person and place names, many of the texts suggest disambiguations of different kinds. Nevertheless, there are still many writing variants of named entities. Furthermore, many texts contain quotations from reference works, some of which are too old to obey the actual orthographic standards.

It is important to notice that the actual data we have to deal with are nevertheless a typical example of the state of the art of documentation in many cultural heritage institutions. Hence, the techniques of content analysis and annotation presented in the following will be of a general utility in many similar projects.

3 Content Analysis: Shallow Parsing and Semantic Representation

The texts contained in the free text fields are encoded with the TEI Lite tag set, supplemented by tags of the module `namesdates` for person and place names. For processing, all texts in the free text fields of a MIDAS file — e.g., the "object" file containing all object descriptions in the "database" — are merged in a single multi-text TEI file. Each text from a data field is represented as a `<text>` element where the text proper without further annotations is contained in its subordinate `<body>` element. The association between the TEI text elements and the orginal MIDAS data fields is assured by unique XML identifiers in `xml:id` attributes. The "raw" text data are transformed automatically into the initial TEI representation in a rather straightforward way by a script. No further internal structuring is provided at this stage; annotations are added by subsequent processing steps.

Shallow parsing for place names and time specifications is based on sets of chunk rules implemented with the Definite Clause Grammar (DCG) formalism[8] which are executed by Prolog. There are grammars for person and place names and for time specifications; these sets of grammar rules define three partial "parsers". For the three parsers there is only one pass, and there is in principle no restriction on the order in which they are applied. The parsing results of each of the parsers are represented as feature structures, which are then converted to TEI tags and inserted into the file by a separate software component. At this stage, there is no recognition and resolution of anaphoric references, such as pronouns. In a second and independent pass, a lookup of person and place names in Name Authority files is executed and the results are collected in local files. There is no filtering applied to the lookup because, at this point, no special knowledge about these resources is available.

3.1 Tagging

First of all, the texts encoded conforming to the TEI guidelines are annotated with word class tags and lemmata (base forms) by a POS tagger. Lemmatisation is very useful in languages with a rich inflectional system, such as German. For POS tagging, we use the Stuttgart TreeTagger[9] with the STTS tagset which provides categories for German words and delimiters.

[5]cf. slide set by Georg Hohmann: `http://www8.informatik.uni-erlangen.de/IMMD8/Services/transdisc/cidoc2008_hohmann.pdf` ; visited 03.12.2008

[6]The actual version of the ISO standard and a lot of accompanying materials can be retrieved from `http://cidoc.ics.forth.gr/` ; visited 03.12.2008.

[7]`http://www8.informatik.uni-erlangen.de/IMMD8/Services/cidoc-crm/` ; visited 05.02.2009

[8]based on previous work by (Tantzen, 2004).

[9]Institute for Automatic Language Processing of the University of Stuttgart. The tagger is available at `http://www.ims.uni-stuttgart.de/projekte/corplex/TreeTagger/DecisionTreeTagger.html` ; visited 03.12.2008.

The resulting TEI tags express morphosyntactic descriptions. Of particular interest are the tags `<w>` for encoding words and `<c>` for individual punctuation marks which are very well suited for encoding tokens: Both can accept an attribute `type` for the determination of the word or character class. Lemmata are encoded with the attribute `lemma`.

3.2 Time Specifications

The "temporal" grammar/parser recognizes a broad variety of temporal expressions built up from days, weeks, months, seasons of the year, years, decades, and centuries.[10] Time specifications may be given as absolute or relative.

Absolute time specifications describe unique time points or intervals on the time line, such as calendar dates (e.g. *28. August 1749*) and open or closed time spans (e.g. *bis 1832*, up to 1832). Furthermore, modifying particles are recognized, e.g. *Mitte 1749* (midyear 1749) or *Ende März 1832* (end of March 1832).

To determine the missing data in relative time specifications, such as *drei Wochen später* (three weeks later), a kind of anaphoric resolution method is applied. Therefore, we keep track of all occurences of temporal expressions. For resolution, we choose the most recently mentioned at the appropriate level (day, month, year).

3.3 Places

The normal case of place specifications in the goldsmith corpus consists of a geographic place name or a preposition followed by a place name. In some cases there are also enumerations of place names. We distinguish between a named entity and the corresponding linguistic phrase. Named entities are looked up in a local dictionary which is built from entries in Name Authorities.

Before lexical lookup, a procedure is executed which prevents the annotation of lower case words as named entities. It implements the simple heuristics that — even composite — named entities are designated by words beginning with a capital letter, but not each word beginning with a capital letter is a named entity as in English. In German, a noun must be written with its first letter in upper case.

Each named entity is associated with one out of ten geographical types to avoid aggregations of incompatible types as in *die Städte München und Berlin und Finnland* (the cities Munich, Berlin and Finland). On the other hand, certain words such as city, town, settlement, etc. are associated with such a type ("city") to be used as a constraint on subsequent proper nouns.

3.4 Persons

Parsing of person names is much more difficult because they are more complex and there is a considerably larger variation than with place names. Whereas, usually, composite place names are lexicalized, this is not a real option for person names. Every person in German speaking countries has at least one first and one surname, optionally amended by further forenames, appellations of nobility or ancestry or generation. We do not regard titles and forms of address such as *König* (king) or *Herr* (Mister) as parts of names — in spite of the fact that according to German law the title of *Doktor* (doctor) is a part of the name.

For name parsing, the constituents of names are divided into four categories: forenames, surnames, copula, and generation appellations. The class of copula subsumes many particles which serve as predicates of nobility or ancestry, e.g. *von*, *van der* or French/Spanish/Italian *de la*. The category of generation appellations contains words and numberings to distinguish persons with the same name, e.g. *Karl V.*, *Albrecht Dürer* ***der Ältere***.

There are several sources of ambiguities with person names the grammar has to deal with, as well w.r.t. the correct interpretation of their parts as regarding their reference:

- Persons are often referenced not by their full name, but only by their first or surname.
- Many first names may also occur as surnames.
- Many surnames are also names of professions or places.
- There are several standards of equal range for the ordering of name parts.
- The use of a comma to separate surname and first name can be confused with an enumeration and vice versa.

Therefore we use dictionaries for the four categories of name parts. There are words, which may be members of several categories, if there are several possibilities of interpretation. The dictionaries for generation appellations and copula are

[10] The actual text corpus does not contain time of day expressions.

small and have been assembled manually. For first and surnames, several name lists were compiled into one dictionary file from lists available via Name Authorities and also from the WWW.

To recognize person names containing very rare first and surnames, as well as writing variants which are not contained in the lexicon, we use a system of syntactic and semantic cues — based on statistical analyses of the texts — which indicate the occurence of a name at a specific location (cf. table).

syntax of the trigger	Example
profession name	Goldschmied Samuel Klemm
appellation name	Frau Martha
preposition relation name	mit Meister Silvester
possessive pron. rel. name	Seine Tochter Katharina
relation `des/der` *name*	Tochter des Christian Mahler
relation `von` *name*	Sohn von Peter v. Quickelberg
relation : *name*	Lehrling: Lang, Joh. Christoph

Table 1: Rules for person name triggers. Words to be inserted for *profession*, *appellation* and *relation* are taken from hand-made lexica.

Statistical analysis of the goldsmith corpus has given clear evidence for three groups of words whose occurrence indicates an immediate following person name: Appellations of professions, appellations plus titles, and relations between persons. A relation between persons is regarded as a cue only if certain particles occur immediately before or after it. The word sequence *"Tochter von"* (daughter of) is a good example of such a cue for a subsequent person name.

In a first step, the name parts and the cues are labelled separately. In a second pass, whenever a cue or a name part is encountered, an algorithm to assemble the parts into complete person names is run. It tries to match the current word sequence with different patterns of name parts which constitute valid person names, i.e. it applies different finite state machines[11] to the word sequence. The longest sequence recognized by a finite state machine is assumed to be a name (see Table 2).

3.5 Name Authorities

To achieve a normalization of appellations, person and place names are looked up in name authorities. There are several authorities, none of which can claim completeness, and each has its

Pattern	Example
s	Jamnitzer
$s\ g$	Jamnitzer II
$f^+\ s$	Hans Jamnitzer
$f^+\ g\ c\ s$	*Hans II von Jamnitzer
$f^+\ g\ s$	Hans II Jamnitzer
$f^+\ c\ s$	*Hans von Jamnitzer
$f^+\ g$	Hans II
f^+	Hans
$s\ ,\ f^+\ g$	Jamnitzer, Hans II
$s\ ,\ f^+\ c$	*Jamnitzer, Hans von
$s\ ,\ f^+\ g\ c$	*Jamnitzer, Hans II von
$s\ ,\ f^+$	Jamnitzer, Hans

Table 2: Recognized name patterns with examples showing the name of the goldsmith "Hans II Jamnitzer". `s` stands for surname, `f` for forename, `c` for copula and `g` for generation particle. The '+' sign expresses one or more occurences; the asterisk indicates that the name has been modified to fit the pattern with "von".

strengths and weaknesses. Up to now, we have used the following interfaces — however, further interfaces are in preparation: BGN: Board on Geographic Names (German places File)[12], Diskus "Geographie-Datei" (distributed with MIDAS)[13], Orbis Latinus (Graesse)[14], Getty TGN (Thesaurus of Geographic Names)[15], PKNAD (Person Names) by prometheus e.V.[16], and Getty ULAN (United List of Artist Names)[17]

There are two modes of use for name authorities in the process of named entity recognition:

1. Decision making: The data are used as dictionaries for the person name and place name parsers.

2. Enrichment with metadata in a second phase once the named entities are identified.

As there are not yet unique formats and inter-

[11] Finite State Machines are formal automata which recognize regular expression patterns; i.e., both notions are equivalent.

[12] `http://earth-info.nga.mil/gns/html/namefiles.htm` ; visited 17.12.2008

[13] `http://museum.zib.de/museumsvokabular/index.php?main=download` ; visited 17.12.2008

[14] `http://www.columbia.edu/acis/ets/Graesse/contents.html` ; visited 17.12.2008

[15] `http://www.getty.edu/research/conducting_research/vocabularies/tgn/` ; visited 17.12.2008

[16] `http://www.prometheus-bildarchiv.de/index.php?id=56\&L=0\&skin=0` ; visited 17.12.2008

[17] `http://www.getty.edu/research/conducting_research/vocabularies/ulan/` ; visited 17.12.2008

faces for the mentioned name authorities, we implemented a querying interface for each name authority in both modes with the exception of the Getty vocabularies. These are not used directly as dictionaries, but only for metadata enrichment, because the data must be retrieved place by place from individual web pages due to the lack of an appropriate API.

3.5.1 Name Authorities as Dictionaries

Name authorities can be directly accessed through the dictionary interfaces of the place and person name parsers. To accelerate the search for entries, the retrieved data are stored in local dictionary files, one for each name authority. The dictionary files can be generated either during the recognition process or off-line. To keep the local data up to date, the generation process should to be repeated from time to time, at least for some of the mentioned resources.

3.5.2 Name Authorities for Metadata Harvesting

Metadata harvesting has been implemented as a separate process; it consists of the search for annotations of named entities in the TEI files, of querying name authorities and collecting the metadata through special interfaces, encoding in an appropriate format and storing in local files. We do not rank name authorities and the content of the metadata; its structure and degree of detail are taken as retrieved. However, with each data set the list of IDs of the tagged findings in the TEI file is stored.

3.6 TEI-Encoding of Named Entities

Temporal expressions are encoded with the `<date>` tag. For the attributes, the distinction between time spans and time points is represented by the attributes `from` and `to`, or the attribute `when`, resp.

The tag `<placeName>` is used to annotate place expressions as a whole. To label the named entities contained within, the TEI module `namesdates` provides six tags according to its geographical type: `<district>`, `<settlement>`, `<region>`, `<country>`, `<bloc>` und `<geogName>`; for some of them there may be a refinement by means of the ten geographic types mentioned in 3.3 with the attribute `type`.

For person names, the TEI tag `<persName>` and several subtags are defined, among which `<surname>`, `<forename>`, `<nameLink>` and `<genName>` correspond exactly to the name parts presented above.

3.7 Evaluation Results

The three partial parsers are executed in sequential order. The best results were obtained in the order time – person – place:

On the goldsmith corpus with a test set of about 2000 word types, a precision of 81.8% and a recall of 72.6% was achieved with the described level of granularity, i.e., accounting for the distinction of first and last names and geographic types.

If these distinctions are dropped, as in many other systems, precision increases to 83.0% and recall to 82.6%.

A separate evaluation of the parsers (in parentheses: with distinctions) showed for

- time: precision 89.0% and recall 92.1%,
- person: precision 74.4% (71.6%) and recall 87.0% (75.5%),
- place: precision 78.9% (69.1%) and recall 76.9% (71.7%),

Depending on the choice of name authorities used for lexicon generation, and due to a high degree of ambiguity, too many words may be classified as place names. For this reason, BGN has been left out, because it led to a considerable decrease of precision and a slight increase of recall.

4 Building Blocks for Event Recognition

With parsing results for person and place names and time specifications, we have a first-level partial semantic representation of text chunks, which could be combined into larger representation structures. However, considering the characteristics of the given free texts and the state of the art in computational linguistics, it would be presumptuous to aim at a deep semantic analysis. Nevertheless, under the assumption of compositionality, i.e., the assumption that semantic representations of larger units are to be composed from those of their parts in a systematic way, it is possible to assemble partial semantic representations. In particular, we are interested in identifying events and the involved actors, objects, and instruments. Event recognition in texts has been an active research area in recent years, in particu-

```
<?xml version="1.0" encoding="UTF-8" standalone="no"?>
<TEI>
  <teiHeader>
    ...
  </teiHeader>
  <text>
    <group>
      <text xml:id="kue00020e00029">
        <body>
    Er ist offensichtlich identisch mit dem Ornamentstecher
<persName xml:id="persName4815108">
  <forename>Theodor</forename>
  <surname>B.</surname>
</persName>
    und stammte wie
<persName xml:id="persName6059828">
  <surname>Bang</surname>
    ,
  <forename>Hieronymus</forename>
</persName>
<placeName type="zone" xml:id="placeName12514145">
    aus
  <settlement type="stadt">Osnabr&uuml;ck</settlement>
</placeName>
    (Verwandtschaft?) Kein Eintrag in den Eheb&uuml;chern
<date from="1600-01-01" to="1699-12-31" xml:id="date33491090">
    des 17. Jhs.
</date>,
    kein Eintrag im Totenbuch St.
<placeName type="zone" xml:id="placeName3113238">
  <district type="stadtteil">Sebald</district>
</placeName>
    bzw.
<placeName type="zone" xml:id="placeName9131644">
  <district type="stadtteil">Lorenz</district></placeName>
    bis
<date from="1623-01-01" to="1630-12-31" xml:id="date24591544">
    1623/30
</date>.
<date from="1611-01-01" to="1611-12-31" xml:id="date22562823">
    Von 1611
</date>
    stammt eine von
<persName xml:id="persName5006112"><surname>Bang</surname></persName>
    gestochene Ansicht
 <placeName type="zone" xml:id="placeName4837279">
    von
 <settlement type="stadt">Bamberg</settlement></placeName>.
 <persName xml:id="persName7446303">
   <forename>Balthasar</forename> <surname>Keimox</surname>
 </persName>
    verlegte von ihm eine Folge von
    12 Stichvorlagen mit reichem Arabeskenwerk.
        </body>
      </text>
    </group>
  </text>
</TEI>
```


Figure 1: Parsing result: annotated text in TEI encoding. (Layout has been rearranged for readability.)

lar in combination with text mining.[18] In previous work (Fischer et al., 1996; Bücher et al., 2002), we augmented a chart-based chunk parser with an incremental construction procedure for (partial) Discourse Representation Structures (DRSs). DRSs are semantic representations which contain a list of discourse referents, introduced by named entities or definite noun phrases, and a body, which consists of a possibly complex logical form representing the meaning of the given part of speech[19]. For events, we use a neo-Davidsonian representation, i.e., the corresponding verb is a one-place predicate whose argument is a discourse referent representing an event, conjoined with binary relations for the thematic roles. For example, the sentence *"Albrecht Dürer painted a self-portrait in 1500 in Nuremberg"* would get a semantic representation in which — extremely simplified — e would be the discourse referent for the event, *paint(e)* the representation of the event, and *actor(e,a)*, *object(e,s)*, *time(e,1500)*, etc. constitute the body, where a and s are the discourse referents for the artist and the self-portrait, resp. DRSs are reaching beyond sentence limits and can in principle be combined into larger and larger discourse structures. Therefore, they are appropriate representations on which reference resolution mechanisms, such as those described in (Fischer et al., 1996) can be built. In our current work, a central activity is to port this method and its implementation to the museum documentation domain and enrich it by collocational analysis as in (Smith, 2002).

The representation of events is not only an extremely important key to content analysis, but also the pivot which connects various objects, persons, places, with each other, making a variety of connections explicit, which are implicitly contained in the data fields and free texts of records of different types. It, therefore, becomes an obvious goal to enrich such relational structures with further information elements from other cultural heritage resources — beyond name authorities. In our particular application, access to Getty's Art and Architecture Thesaurus (AAT), to other museum and collection databases or online auction catalogs would be obvious. Unfortunately, many of these resources use idiosyncratic data formats just as MIDAS mentioned above. At best, they refer to a formal representation of their respective domain, in terms of a so-called "formal domain ontology", a representative hierarchical structure of concepts, properties and constraints of the domain. However, to satisfy the desideratum of linking diverse data collections, an intermediate level of interoperability is required. A well proven approach for such information integration tasks is to link the different domain ontologies to a generic reference ontology, which contains just the fundamental and most general concepts and properties for a wide variety of applications. In fact, for the field of cultural heritage, CIDOC's Conceptual Reference Model (CRM) is such a reference ontology. It is worthwhile to notice that, among other things, the CRM emphasizes the event-driven perspective, in fact, events are the glue in CRM which connects all documentation elements. As a first step, we have already implemented a generator for CRM instances from TEI-conformant texts with named entity annotations.

5 Transdisciplinary Aspects

Coming back to our project on goldsmith art documentation, we recognize clues in the data, which point beyond the domain of cultural history: there are goblets and centerpieces (epergnes) showing sculptered animals, such as lizards and beetles. Two of the documented objects exhibit a beautiful stag beetle, which induced interesting questions about those insects, not only on their iconographic significance, but also on their determination and classification in biology, the distribution of species, etc. This illustrates that there is a need to connect with further knowledge sources, such as resources from biology, biodiversity research, etc. For example, we may want to consult a database such as BIODAT, maintained by the natural history museum Koenig in Bonn. Considering the completely different scientific background and the different perspectives in description, this task seems to be very ambitious, to say the least. Whereas the stag beetle in the foot of the goblet is described in terms of art history and metallurgy, we find a completely different description of a pinned stag beetle in the BIODAT data base. We may be lucky to identify it there if we know the precise species name in advance, but in many cases, there is a significant chance that the match-

[18]To quote just one prominent example, cf. the TERQAS (Time and Event Recognition for Question Answering) Symposium, 2002, `http://www.timeml.org/site/terqas/index.html` ; visited 05.02.2009

[19]cf. (Kamp and Reyle, 1993)

ing task will fail. At this point in time, we can only provide a sketch in terms of an example how we would approach this challenge. But it seems obvious if we could find a general way to connect to different description systems, we would approach the long-term goal of an "epistemic web".

Recent efforts showed that there is in fact a way to a solution, indicated by the term "transdisciplinarity"; first results have been presented at the first meeting of the CIDOC working group on "Transdisciplinary Approaches in Documentation"[20]. Originating from philosophy of science (Mittelstrass, 2002), transdisciplinarity concentrates on problems, which cannot be solved within a single disciplinary framework. It takes a new view on the unity of science, focussing on scientific rationality, not systems. Taking into account that for all sciences there are common elements in the practice of argumentation and justification, transdisciplinarity is a research principle in the first place. Its emphasis on rational language use in science offers a clue to the field of documentation; as a starting point, our methodological focus is first of all on data integration . Taking into account that transdisciplinarity addresses the practice of research, this framework should support an action and event perspective on a generic level, i.e. for the tasks of classification, representation, annotation, linking, etc.

In fact, we claim that the CIDOC CRM can play the role of such a transdisciplinary framework; at least for the stag beetle on goblets and still life paintings, some other insects and also birds on drawings and paintings, the modelling task has already been performed successfully. For the birds — hooded crows in Dutch winter scenes in Brueghel paintings — our transdisciplinary modelling effort provided a nice result for biodiversity research as a side effect: During the "little ice age" hooded crows lived in Western Europe, whereas today they can only be found east of the Elbe river.

Acknowledgments

The authors are grateful for valuable hints and discussions to Siegfried Krause, Georg Hohmann, Karl-Heinz Lampe, and Bernhard Schiemann and to the anonymous reviewers for valuable suggestions.

[20]at the CIDOC 2008 conference; online materials are available via `http://www8.informatik.uni-erlangen.de/IMMD8/Services/transdisc/` ; visited 03.12.2008.

References

Kerstin Bücher, Günther Goerz, and Bernd Ludwig. 2002. Corega Tabs: Incremental semantic composition. In Günther Goerz and et al., editors, *KI-2002 Workshop on Applications of Description Logics, Proceedings*, volume 63 of *CEUR Workshop Proceedings*, Aachen, September. Gesellschaft für Informatik e.V.

Martin Doerr. 2003. The CIDOC Conceptual Reference Model: an ontological approach to semantic interoperability of metadata. *AI Magazine*, 24(3):75–92, September.

Ingrid Fischer, Bernd Geistert, and Günther Goerz. 1996. Incremental semantics construction and anaphora resolution using Lambda-DRT. In S. Botley and J. Glass, editors, *Proceedings of DAARC-96 — Discourse Anaphora and Anaphor Resolution Colloquium*, pages 235–244, Lancaster, July.

Günther Goerz, Martin Oischinger, and Bernhard Schiemann. 2008. An Implementation of the CIDOC Conceptual Reference Model (4.2.4) in OWL-DL. In *Proceedings of the 2008 Annual Conference of CIDOC — The Digital Curation of Cultural Heritage*, pages 1–14, Athens, Benaki Museum, September 15–18.

Lutz Heusinger. 1989. *Marburger Informations-, Dokumentations- und Administrations-System (MIDAS) / [1,2]*. Saur, München.

Nancy Ide and Jean Veronis, editors. 1995. *Text Encoding Initiative. Background and Context.* Kluwer, Dordrecht. Also in: Computers and the Humanities. Vol. 29, No. 1–3 (1995).

Hans Kamp and Uwe Reyle. 1993. *From Discourse to Logic*. Kluwer, Dordrecht.

Jürgen Mittelstrass. 2002. Transdisciplinarity — new structures in science. In *Innovative Structures in Basic Research. Ringberg-Symposium, 4–7 October 2000*, number 5 in Max Planck Forum, pages 43–54, München.

David A. Smith. 2002. Detecting events with date and place information in unstructured text. In *Proceedings of the 2nd ACM+IEEE Joint Conference on Digital Libraries*, pages 191–196, Portland, OR.

Regine Stein and Erin Coburn. 2008. CDWA Lite and museumdat: New developments in metadata standards for cultural heritage information. In *Proceedings of the 2008 Annual Conference of CIDOC*, Athens, September 15–18.

Svenja Tantzen. 2004. Ein Prologparser für temporale und lokale Ausdrücke in einem 'Geosem-System' für das Deutsche. Technical report, Friedrich-Alexander-Universität Erlangen-Nürnberg, Philosophische Fakultät II, Erlangen. Master Thesis.

An intelligent authoring environment for abstract semantic representations of cultural object descriptions

Stasinos Konstantopoulos and **Vangelis Karkaletsis** and **Dimitris Bilidas**
Institute of Informatics & Telecommunications
NCSR 'Demokritos', Greece
{konstant,vangelis,dbilid}@iit.demokritos.gr

Abstract

In this paper we describe an authoring environment for the creation of cultural-domain ontologies and the associated linguistic and profile annotations, for dynamically generating adaptable natural-language descriptions of the cultural objects in the ontology. Adaptation is achieved at the expense of considerable authoring effort, since it relies on providing numerical parameters for each ontological entity. To assist the authoring process, we provide an intelligent authoring back-end that completes manually authored models by inferring missing values. This intelligent authoring support facility, combined with immediate previews, can considerably reduce the effort required to create a fully functional model as the author can iterate through cycles of providing information, previewing the generated text, and only elaborating the model where the text is unsatisfactory.

1 Introduction

Cultural heritage organizations create and maintain repositories of (digital representations of) artifacts, including extensive semantic knowledge and meta-data about the cultural objects in the collection. Such semantic repositories are typically seen as an opportunity to catalogue, index, and classify the cultural content, for the purpose of providing semantic *searching* and *browsing* facilities to professional users as well as to the general public.

In this article we discuss another unique opportunity that cultural heritage repositories offer: the opportunity to automatically generate adaptable and customizable *textual descriptions* of the cultural objects for a variety of audiences and purposes.

More specifically, we present ELEON, an authoring environment for creating abstract conceptual representations of cultural heritage object descriptions, as well as the linguistic and profiling models necessary to realize those into concrete natural-language descriptions exploiting natural language generation technology. The advantages of this approach, as opposed to directly authoring natural language descriptions, are manifold:

- Abstract descriptions constitute machine-readable and reusable models of the cultural heritage collection. Besides deriving natural language descriptions, such models can be used for the semantic indexing and searching of the collection. This can also be seen from the reverse perspective: the natural language descriptions can be derived from existing conceptual models created for the purpose of semantic indexing and searching.
- The conceptual descriptions are realized using domain-independent, reusable linguistic models. By clearly separating the conceptual and linguistic models, the same conceptual descriptions can be realized in different languages and the same linguistic models can be used to realize descriptions of different collections.
- The dynamic generation of the description is driven by profiles that personalize the descriptions for different audiences, but also adapt them to different contexts and situations.

ELEON provides great flexibility in finely parametrizing how the generated descriptions are adapted to different audiences and situations. Furthermore, the authoring environment is backed by Artificial Intelligence tools that assist the author

Proceedings of the EACL 2009 Workshop on Language Technology and Resources for Cultural Heritage, Social Sciences, Humanities, and Education –LaTeCH – SHELT&R 2009, pages 10–17,
Athens, Greece, 30 March 2009.

by automatically inferring missing profile parameters, alleviating the burden of explicitly providing all necessary details for large numbers of objects.

Although the system can be used in a variety of domains and Human-Computer interaction applications, it is particularly pertinent to cultural heritage content, which is interesting for wide ranges of age groups, levels of expertise, cultural and educational backgrounds, situations and contexts, emphasising the need for personalized and custom-tailored text.

In the rest of this article we first set the background by describing the authoring environment and particularly the way in which it can be used to create the conceptual model of the collection and populate it with data (Section 2) and then proceed to to describe how adaptation parameters are represented and used by human-computer interaction systems (Section 3). We then focus on the main contribution of this paper by describing the intelligence mechanism behind the environment (Section 4), discuss related work (Section 5), and conclude (Section 6).

2 Authoring Domain Ontologies

ELEON enables its authors—i.e., persons that have domain expertise but no technological expertise—to create a new application domain, defining the ontology of the new domain, as well as the corresponding language resources and the profiling models. All these elements are used by a natural language generation (NLG) engine in order to derive natural language descriptions from the conceptual representations in the ontology. The environment also enables authors to generate text previews using the NLG engine in order to examine the effect of their updates to the domain ontology, the language resources and the profiling parameters.

Concerning the language resources, these affect the content and the surface form of the derived texts, leading to more varied texts and contain entries for nouns and verbs for each supported language. With regard to the profiling parameters, these are used by ELEON to adapt the generated descriptions to the users' preferences and knowledge.

ELEON ontologies encode domain knowledge in the form of concepts, instances of concepts, (entity types and entities respectively in ELEON terminology), and relations between concepts and instances.

Figure 1 illustrates part of such an ontology that encodes knowledge about the ancient Agora of Athens. This ontology is used in the INDIGO project,[1] implementing a use case where the system guides visitors through an exhibition on the ancient Agora of Athens, introducing the buildings to them before they attend a virtual 3D tour of the Agora hosted at the Foundation of the Hellenic World. The examples used in this paper are drawn from this domain.

In the example of Figure 1, 'stoa-of-attalus', is an instance of the entity type Stoa, a sub-type of Building which is a sub-type of ArchitecturalConstruction, a sub-type of PhysicalObject. Properties and relationships are expressed using fields. For any entity type, it is possible to introduce new fields which then become available to all the entities that belong to that type and its subtypes. In Figure 1, the field locatedIn is introduced at the ArchitecturalConstruction entity type and is defined as a relationship between ArchitecturalConstruction and Place, while the using-period field defines a property of the PhysicalObject entity type. Consequently, all entities of type PhysicalObject and its subtypes, i.e. ArchitecturalConstruction and ArtObject inherit these fields. Furthermore, all the instances of these entity types and their subtypes also inherit these fields.

The proposed system expresses such ontological conceptual models in OWL [11], an ontology representation language that is one of the core semantic web technologies. OWL models can be created from scratch in the authoring tool or imported, facilitating the use of well-established conceptual models in the cultural heritage domain, as almost all can be (or already are) expressed as ontologies. The CIDOC conceptual reference model, for example, also provides an official OWL version.[2] Most other cultural heritage vocabularies, thesauri, and classification schemes using XML or relational database data models are consistent with the *Simple Knowledge Organization System* (SKOS) and can be automatically converted to ontologies.[3]

---

[1]See `http://www.ics.forth.gr/indigo/` and Acknowledgements section.

[2]`http://cidoc.ics.forth.gr/official_release_cidoc.html`

[3]See `http://www.w3.org/2004/02/skos/` about SKOS. A variety of tools exist for converting SKOS data models to, or aligning with,

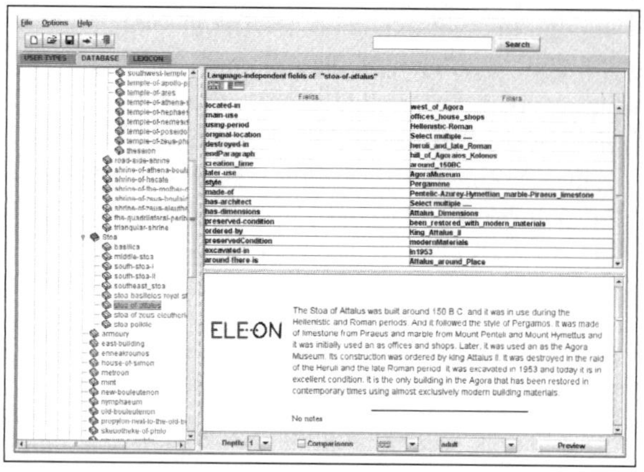

Figure 1: ELEON screen, showing the class hierarchy and the individuals of each class (left), the properties of the currently selected individual (right top), and a preview of the description of the individual (right bottom). The preview language and profile can be seen on (and selected from) the bar at the bottom of the screen.

3 Description Adaptation

Besides modelling the cultural heritage domain itself, ELEON supports annotating the objects, classes, and properties of the domain with adaptation and linguistic information. Such information is used by NLG engines to (a) plan the description that will be generated, adapting it to the current audience and circumstance, and (b) realize the planned description in a particular language.

Realization is based on clause plans (micro-plans) that specify how an ontological property can be expressed in each supported natural language. The author specifies the clause to be generated in abstract terms, by specifying, for example, the verb to be used, the voice and tense of the resulting clause, etc. Similar annotations for instances and classes specify how they should be realized as noun phrases that fill slots in the property-generated clauses. Micro-plan annotations also comprise several other language-specific parameters, such as whether the resulting clause can be aggregated into a longer sentence or not, its voice and tense, and so on, as described in more detail by Androutsopoulos et al. [1], Sect. 3.

Adaptive planning, on the other hand, operates at the abstract level and does not involve specifics of the target language. It is rather aimed at reflecting a *synthetic personality* in the description, as well as *personalizing* it for a particular audience. Adaptation parameters are provided in the form of *profile attributes* that control aspects of the text plan such as how many and which of the facts known about an object should be used to describe it, as discussed in more detail below.

ontological models. See, for example, `http://www.heppnetz.de/projects/skos2gentax/` and `http://annocultor.sourceforge.net/`

3.1 Personalization and personality

The system supports authoring the *adaptation profiles* that control the *dynamic adaptation* of the generated descriptions. Profiles permit the author to specify, for example, that technical vocabulary be used when generating for experts, or that shorter and simpler sentences are generated for children. This is achieved by providing a variety of generation parameters though user profiles, including a numerical *interest* attribute of the properties of the ontology.

Isard et al. [7] describe how interest is used to impose a preference ordering of the properties of ontological entities, controlling which facts will be used when describing each entity. In the work described here, we have extended profiles in two respects:

- by generalizing *interest* into arbitrary, author-defined *profile attributes*; and
- by permitting profile attributes to apply not only to ontological properties, but also to individuals and classes.

Using these extensions, authors can define *personality profiles* for generating text, managing dialogue, and simulating emotional variation in a way that reflects a certain *personality* on behalf of the system.

In the INDIGO project we use these profiles in a human-robot interaction application, where a robotic tour guide that gives the impression of empathizing with the visitor is perceived as more natural and user-friendly. But the methodology is generally interesting in any context of generating descriptions of cultural heritage content, especially if the individual descriptions are aggregated in a tour of the collection. In such contexts, dialogue-management adaptivity can vary the exhibits included in personalized tours and emotional state variation can match the described content and make the tour more engaging and lively.

The way in which personality profiles are used to parametrize dialogue management and simulated emotions are discussed in more detail elsewhere [9], so we shall only briefly outline it here. Emotional variation is achieved by using the personality profile to estimate the *emotional appraisal* of dialogue acts and update the mood and emotional state of artificial agents. Dialogue management is affected both directly, by taking exhibit preference into account when deliberating over dialogue acts, and indirectly, by being influenced by the artificial agent's current mood; and, as already mentioned above, NLG is adapted by using property preference to plan a description

In the Konstantopoulos et al. [9] model, preference is calculated based on a logic model of the robot's personality traits and also on ground facts regarding objective attributes of the content—such as the *importance* of an exhibit—but also subjective attributes that reflect the robot's perception of the content—such as how *interesting* an exhibit is. With the work described here, we alleviate the burden of manually providing all the ground parameters, exploiting the fact that these parameters are strongly inter-related and can, to a large extend, be automatically inferred. More specifically, ELEON backs the profile authoring process by reasoning over manually provided exhibit attributes in order to infer what the values of the missing attributes should be. The author can inspect the explicitly provided as well as the automatically inferred values and make corrections where necessary (Figure 2). Manual corrections trigger a re-estimation of the missing values, so that after each round of corrections the overall model is a closer approximation of the author's intention.

3.2 Representation and interoperability

Linguistic and profile annotations are represented in RDF, the *Resource Description Framework* (RDF) [5]. RDF is a knowledge representation technology built around the concept of using subject-predicate-object triples to describe abstract entities, *resources*. RDF triples assign to their subject resource the property of being related to the object through the predicate resource. Predicates can be *data properties*, in which case their objects are concrete values (numbers, strings, time periods, and so on), or *object properties*, in which case their objects are abstract resources.

Although OWL is not formally defined in RDF, it is defined in such a way that it can be represented within RDF. In fact, the OWL specification

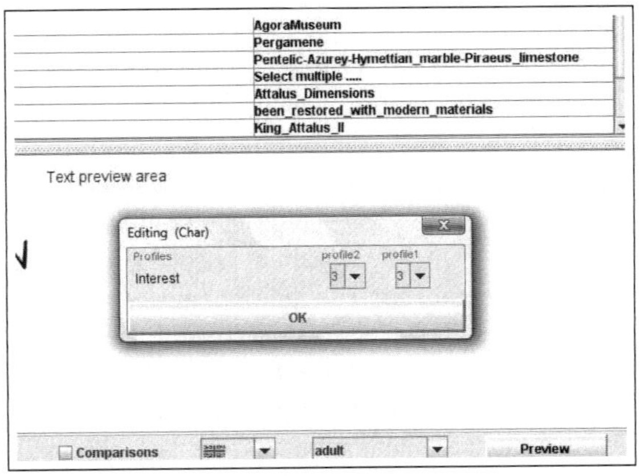

Figure 2: Screen fragment, showing the pop-up window for providing profile attribute values for an exhibit. Automatically inferred attribute values are displayed in red, to stand out from explicitly provided ones which are displayed in black.

itself provides a serialization of OWL ontologies as RDF for transport and data interchange purposes. Since ELEON uses this OWL/RDF representation for the domain ontology, linguistic and profile annotations can be directly represented as RDF triples of extra-ontological properties of the ontological instances.

The RDF vocabulary used defines a property that relates ontological entities (individuals, classes, and properties) with profile attribute nodes that involve:

- the profile to which they are pertinent, e.g., 'expert';
- the attribute, e.g., 'interest' or 'importance'; and
- the numerical value of the attribute for this entity in this profile.

When applied to ontology properties, profile attribute nodes can be further elaborated to apply only to properties of instances of a particular class. For example, one can express that users find it more interesting to know the architectural style when discussing temples than when discussing stoas.

Using RDF is motivated by the usage of OWL to represent the domain ontology as well as the availability of natural language generation (NLG) engines that support it. More specifically, as already discussed, OWL ontologies and RDF annotations can be easily merged in a combined model since OWL ontologies can be expressed in RDF.

An alternative approach would have been to incorporate profile attributes in the OWL ontology. Since profile attributes refer to classes and properties as well as individuals, profile attributes would, then, have to be interpreted as second-order ontological properties. Although second-order constructs can be represented in OWL-Full (the most expressive 'dialect' of OWL), logical inference over OWL-Full ontologies is a challenging and computationally inefficient task. In fact, second-order inference is only supported by research prototypes and only for restricted fragments, often excluding binary second-order predicates (second-order properties).

By contrast, the chosen approach restricts the ontology within the computationally efficient OWL-DL dialect, for which multiple stable and highly optimized inference engines have been developed. Profile attributes are provided as extra-ontological properties, without tying them to a particular logical interpretation. We shall revisit this point in the following section.

The second motivating factor behind RDF profile attributes is interoperability with NLG engines. The RDF vocabulary used to assign linguistic and profile attributes is understood by the NATURALOWL [6] and METHODIUS [10] generation engines (Figure 3).

4 Intelligent Authoring Support

We have previously discussed how profile attributes were not directly incorporated in the domain ontology as second-order statements, but are rather represented as extra-logical RDF annotations. While avoiding forcing a second-order interpretation of profile attributes is a definite advantage from a computational-complexity point of view, this choice leaves profile attributes outside the scope of OWL reasoning tools.

In order to be able to efficiently reason over and draw inferences about profile attributes, we have chosen to interpret profile attributes within *many-valued description logics*. Using description logics has the advantage of direct access to the domain ontology; using many-valued valuations has the advantage of providing a means to represent and reason over numerical values.

This section describes this interpretation and how it is used, after first introducing description logics and many-valued valuations.

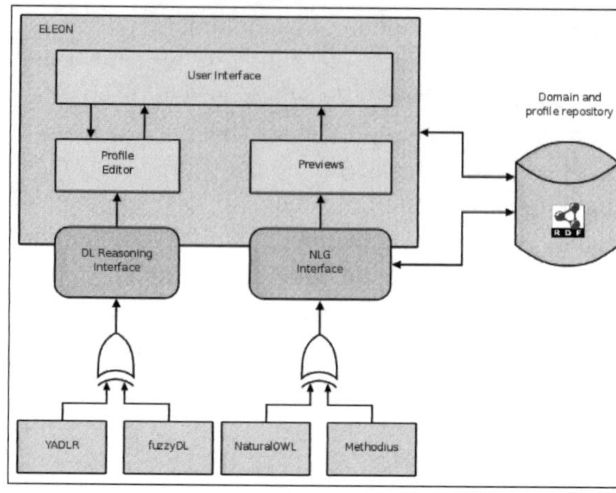

Figure 3: System architecture showing the interfacing with NLG and Inference engines

4.1 Integrating reasoning in ELEON

ELEON specifies a Java interface through which inference results can be requested and retrieved: OWL domain models and RDF profile annotations are passed to an inference engine, which responds with the numerical values of profile attributes for all ontological entities in the domain (individuals, classes, and properties).

ELEON also extends and uses the TransOnto semantic knowledge migration system[4] to perform all the necessary transformations for using many-valued DL reasoners, i.e., transforming the OWL and RDF models into many-valued DL assertions, as well as transforming logical query answers into the numerical profile-attribute values.

Furthermore, as depicted in Figure 3, the implementation includes the necessary API calls for using either of two many-valued DL reasoners, YADLR [8] or FUZZYDL [4]. Support for alternative many-valued DL reasoners can be easily added, by using such reasoners to implement the reasoning API expected by the authoring system.

4.2 Many-valued DL Reasoning

Description Logics (DL) [2] are a family of first-order logics; their main characteristic is *decidability*, attained by being restricted to *concepts* (unary predicates, sets of individuals) and *relations* (binary predicates, sets of pairs of individuals). Of particular importance is the DL called $\mathcal{SHOIN}$, which covers OWL-DL.

[4]See `http://transonto.sourceforge.net/`

DL statements, *concept descriptions*, use logical connectives to define concepts by combining (a) other concepts, and (b) relation constructs that describe the set of individuals that have a certain relation with a certain set of *fillers* (relation objects). Relation descriptions are not supported, and membership in a relation can only be explicitly asserted, except for a limited set of relation axioms such as inversion, subordination, and transitivity. Most DL reasoners also provide limited support for reasoning over concrete domains (numbers, strings, etc.) through *data properties* that relate abstract individual subjects with concrete value objects.

Many-valued logics in general, and consequently many-valued DLs, extend the binary true-false valuations of logical formulae into many-valued numerical valuations, denoting the *degree* to which formulae hold. Such many-valued models receive their semantics not from set theory, as is the case with binary valuations, but from algebraic *norms* that assign semantics to the logical connectives. These norms are used to calculate the degree at which complex logical propositions hold, given the degrees of their constituent elementary propositions.

In the work described here we use *Łukasziewicz-Tarski algebra* to provide many-valued semantics [9, Sect. 3]. Although there is nothing in ELEON itself that forces this choice, Łukasiewicz-Tarski algebra is well-suited to inferring profile attribute values, as it is founded on neither probability nor uncertainty, which would be inappropriate in our case, but on the notion of *relevance*.

4.3 Inferring missing attribute values

Profile attributes of individuals are captured by normalizing in the $[0, 1]$ range and then using the normalized value as a class membership degree. So, for example, if `interesting` is such an attribute of individual exhibits, then an exhibit with a (normalized) interest level of 0.7 is an instance of the Interesting class at a degree of 0.7.

Attributes of classes are reduced to attributes of the members of the class, expressed by a class subsumption assertion at the degree of the attribute. So, if the class of stoas is interesting at a degree of 0.6, this is expressed by asserting that being a member of Stoa implies being a member of Interesting. The implication is asserted at a degree of 0.6, which, under Łukasiewicz-Tarski semantics, means that being a stoa implies being interesting at a loss of 0.4 of a degree. Thus individuals that are members of the Stoa class at a degree of 1.0, are implicitly interesting at a degree of 0.6. Although this is not identical to saying that the class itself is interesting, it clearly captures the intention behind the original RDF annotation.

Ontology Instance	Interesting membership
Doric style	0.8
Ionic style	0.7
Pergamene style	0.3
Attalus	0.9

Table 1: Profile fragment.

Resource	Property	Value
Stoa of Attalus	style	Doric
Stoa of Attalus	style	Ionic
Stoa of Attalus	style	Pergamene
Stoa of Attalus	orderedBy	Attalus

Table 2: Ontology fragment, showing the properties of the 'Stoa of Attalus' instance.

Profile attributes can also characterize properties, like orderedBy, creationEra or style, encoding the information that it might, for example, be more interesting to describe the artistic style of an exhibit rather than provide historical data about it. This is interpreted as the strength of the connection between how interesting an exhibit is, and how interesting its properties are. In other words, if having an interesting filler for style also makes the exhibit interesting, this is taken as an indication that the style relation itself is an interesting one. Formulated in logical terms, having interesting relation fillers implies being interesting, and the implication holds at a degree provided by the interest level of the relation itself.

For example, consider the assertion at 0.8 that the class of things that are related to at least one Interesting instance with the style property, are themselves Interesting and the assertion at 0.4 that the class of things that are related to at least one Interesting instance with the orderedBy property, are themselves Interesting.

Given a profile fragment like the one in Table 1 and a domain ontology including the factual information in Table 2, 'Stoa of Attalus' has an interesting style at a degree of 0.8, which is the maximum among the three architectural styles found in the stoa (Doric, Ionic, and Pergamene). Since style fillers transfer interest at a loss of 0.2, style contributes 0.6 to the stoa's Interesting-ness. By contrast, the filler of orderedBy (which is more interesting in this profile than any of the architectural styles) only contributes 0.3 of a degree, because orderedBy is annotated as uninteresting and interest transfers across it at a heavy loss.

We have so far discussed how to infer profile attribute values for the individuals of the domain. Classes and relations receive the value of the minimal instance of the class (relation). That is to say, the individual (pair of individuals) for which nothing else is known, except that it is a member of the class (relation).

As an example, consider a DoricBuilding class which is a subclass of Building that only admits instances that have a style relation with 'Doric'. The minimal instance of this class is a member of Interesting through having an interesting property as discussed above, even though nothing else is known about it. This membership degree in Interesting is taken to be an attribute of the class itself rather than any one of its members, and is used as the attribute value for the class itself.

For relations, two minimal instances of the relation's domain and range are created. The attribute value for the property is the degree of the implication that having this property makes the domain individual have the attribute. For example, in order to infer how interesting the property devotedTo is, we first observe that it relates Temple instances with MythicalPerson instances, and create bare instances of these two classes. The implication that having a devotedTo relation to an Interesting individual leads to being member of Interesting holds to a degree that can be calculated, given the Interesting degrees of the Temple and MythicalPerson instances involved in the relation. The degree of the implication is then used as the value of the `interesting` attribute.

5 Related Work

ELEON is based on the authoring tool described by Androutsopoulos et al. [1], which was also targeted at creating ontologies for generating personalized descriptions of the individuals in the ontology. ELEON inherits from that tool the idea of separating the abstract ontological relations from the concrete linguistic information, facilitating the easy reuse of the ontological information to generate descriptions in multiple languages, as well as using an external NLG engine to provide previews of the descriptions from within the authoring environment.

The system presented here extends a previous version of ELEON [3], which supports using an external DL reasoner to catch logical errors by checking the consistency of the authored ontology. In the work described here, the intelligence behind the tool is substantially extended by using logical inference to *predict* values that have not been explicitly entered by the user, alleviating the need to manually provide large volumes of numerical data.

A parallel line of development of the original Androutsopoulos et al. tool is based on the Protégé ontology authoring and management environment.[5] Galanis and Androutsopoulos [6] developed a Protégé plug-in that builds upon the extensive ontology authoring features of Protégé to provide an environment for creating cultural heritage ontologies and the associated linguistic and profiling annotations. It does not, however, offer the flexibility to define new profile attributes as ELEON does, and is restricted to specifying the level of interest of the various ontological entities. Furthermore, it only uses logic inference to catch ontological inconsistencies in a manner similar to that described by Bilidas et al. [3] without any prediction facilities.

6 Conclusion

In this article we have presented an authoring environment for the creation of domain ontologies and the associated linguistic and profile annotations. Annotated ontologies can be used to automatically generate natural-language descriptions of the entities of the ontology, dynamically adapting the generation engine to the audience and context of the description.

The advantages of using ELEON instead of generic knowledge tools, such as Protégé, stem from the ability to couple ELEON with external engines that provide important conveniences to the author. More specifically, ELEON can invoke a natural language generation engine in order to display previews of the description based on the information currently provided about an object. Furthermore, logical inference is used to provide an intel-

[5] See `http://protege.stanford.edu/`

ligent authoring back-end that completes the current model by inferring missing values based on what has already been provided.

This intelligent authoring support facility, combined with the immediate previews, can considerably reduce the effort required to create a fully functional model as the author can iterate through cycles of providing information, previewing the generated text, and only elaborating the model where the text is unsatisfactory. This iterative process converges to satisfactory descriptions much faster than having to manually enter all adaptation parameters, especially for large and complex domains.

In the context of the XENIOS project,[6] the previous version of ELEON has been evaluated by curators of the Foundation of the Hellenic World, who used it to create an ontology of the buildings, rooms, and exhibitions of the Foundation. In the context of creating the Agora of Athens ontology and annotations for INDIGO, we are planning to extend this evaluation to include the new intelligent authoring features.

Acknowledgements

The work described here is supported by the FP6-IST project INDIGO[7] which aims to advance human-robot interaction methodology and technology, enabling robots to perceive natural human behaviour, as well as making them act in ways that are more familiar to humans. The authors also wish to acknowledge the help of the colleagues from the Foundation of the Hellenic World who used ELEON to create the initial version of the ontology for the ancient Agora of Athens.

References

[1] Ion Androutsopoulos, Jon Oberlander, and Vangelis Karkaletsis. 2007. Source authoring for multilingual generation of personalised object descriptions. *Journal of Natural Language Engineering*, 13(3):191–233.

[2] Franz Baader, Ian Horrocks, and Ulrike Sattler. 2003. Description logics as ontology languages for the semantic web. In Steffen Staab and Rudi Studer, editors, *Lecture Notes in Artificial Intelligence*. Springer Verlag.

[3] Dimitris Bilidas, Maria Theologou, and Vangelis Karkaletsis. 2007. Enriching OWL ontologies with linguistic and user-related annotations: the ELEON system. In *Proc. 19th IEEE Intl. Conf. on Tools with Artificial Intelligence (ICTAI-2007), Patras, Greece, Oct. 2007*. IEEE Computer Society.

[4] Fernando Bobillo and Umberto Straccia. 2008. fuzzyDL: an expressive fuzzy Description Logic reasoner. In *Proceedings of the 2008 International Conference on Fuzzy Systems (FUZZ-08)*.

[5] Dan Brickley and R. V. Guha. 2004. RDF Primer. W3C Recommendation.

[6] Dimitris Galanis and Ion Androutsopoulos. 2007. Generating multilingual descriptions from linguistically annotated OWL ontologies: the NaturalOWL system. In *Proceedings of the 11th European Workshop on Natural Language Generation (ENLG 2007), Schloss Dagstuhl, Germany*, pages 143–146.

[7] Amy Isard, Jon Oberlander, Ion Androutsopoulos, and Colin Matheson. 2003. Speaking the users' languages. *IEEE Intelligent Systems*, 18(1):40–45.

[8] Stasinos Konstantopoulos and Georgios Apostolikas. 2007. Fuzzy-DL reasoning over unknown fuzzy degrees. In *Proc. Intl. IFIP Workshop of Semantic Web and Web Semantics (IFIP-SWWS 07)*, Nov. 2007, Vilamoura, Portugal. LNCS 4806, Springer, Berlin/Heidelberg.

[9] Stasinos Konstantopoulos, Vangelis Karkaletsis, and Colin Matheson. 2008. Robot personality: Representation and externalization. In *Proceedings of Intl. Workshop on Computational Aspects of Affective and Emotional Interaction (CAFFEi 08)*, Patras, Greece, July 2008.

[10] Matthew Marge, Amy Isard, and Johanna Moore. 2008. Creation of a new domain and evaluation of comparison generation in a natural language generation system. In *Proceedings of the Fifth International Language Generation Conference (INLG08), June 2008, Salt Fork, Ohio, USA*.

[11] Michael K. Smith, Chris Welty, and Deborah L. McGuinness. 2004. OWL web ontology language. W3C Recommendation.

[6] See `http://www.ics.forth.gr/xenios/` (in Greek)

[7] See `http://www.ics.forth.gr/indigo/`

Multiple sequence alignments in linguistics

Jelena Prokić
University of Groningen
The Netherlands
j.prokic@rug.nl

Martijn Wieling
University of Groningen
The Netherlands
m.b.wieling@rug.nl

John Nerbonne
University of Groningen
The Netherlands
j.nerbonne@rug.nl

Abstract

In this study we apply and evaluate an iterative pairwise alignment program for producing multiple sequence alignments, ALPHAMALIG (Alonso et al., 2004), using as material the phonetic transcriptions of words used in Bulgarian dialectological research. To evaluate the quality of the multiple alignment, we propose two new methods based on comparing each column in the obtained alignments with the corresponding column in a set of gold standard alignments. Our results show that the alignments produced by ALPHAMALIG correspond well with the gold standard alignments, making this algorithm suitable for the automatic generation of multiple string alignments. Multiple string alignment is particularly interesting for historical reconstruction based on sound correspondences.

1 Introduction

Our cultural heritage is studied today not only in museums, libraries, archives and their digital portals, but also through the genetic and cultural lineaments of living populations. Linguists, population geneticists, archaeologists, and physical and cultural anthropologists are all active in researching cultural heritage on the basis of material that may or may not be part of official cultural heritage archives. The common task is that of understanding the histories of the peoples of the world, especially their migrations and contacts. To research and understand linguistic cultural heritage we require instruments which are sensitive to its signals, and, in particular sensitive to signals of common provenance. The present paper focuses on pronunciation habits which have been recognized to bear signals of common provenance for over two hundred years (since the work of Sir William Jones).

We present work in a research line which seeks to submit pronunciation data to phylogenetic analysis (Gray and Atkinson, 2003) and which requires an alignment of the (phonological) segments of cognate words. We focus in this paper on evaluating the quality of multi-aligned pronunciations.

In bioinformatics, sequence alignment is a way of arranging DNA, RNA or protein sequences in order to identify regions of similarity and determine evolutionary, functional or structural similarity between the sequences. There are two main types of string alignment: pairwise and multiple string alignment. Pairwise string alignment methods compare two strings at a time and cannot directly be used to obtain multiple string alignment methods (Gusfield, 1997, 343-344). In multiple string alignment all strings are aligned and compared at the same time, making it a good technique for discovering patterns, especially those that are weakly preserved and cannot be detected easily from sets of pairwise alignments. Multiple string comparison is considered to be *the holy grail* of molecular biology (Gusfield, 1997, 332):

> It is the most critical cutting-edge tool for *extracting and representing* biologically important, yet faint or widely dispersed, commonalities from a set of strings.

Multiple string comparison is not new in linguistic research. In the late 19th century the Neogrammarians proposed the hypothesis of the regularity of sound change. According to THE NEOGRAMMARIAN HYPOTHESIS sound change occurs regularly and uniformly whenever the appropriate phonetic environment is encountered (Campbell, 2004). Ever since, the understanding of sound change has played a major role in the comparative method that is itself based on the simultaneous comparison of different languages, i.e. lists of cognate terms from the related languages. The correct analysis of sound changes

Proceedings of the EACL 2009 Workshop on Language Technology and Resources for Cultural Heritage, Social Sciences, Humanities, and Education –LaTeCH – SHELT&R 2009, pages 18–25,
Athens, Greece, 30 March 2009.

requires the simultaneous examination of corresponding sounds in order to compare hypotheses about their evolution. Alignment identifies which sounds correspond. Historical linguists align the sequences manually, while we seek to automate this process.

In recent years there has been a strong focus in historical linguistics on the introduction of quantitative methods in order to develop tools for the comparison and classification of languages. For example, in his PhD thesis, Kondrak (2002) presents algorithms for the reconstruction of proto-languages from cognates. Warnow et al. (2006) applied methods taken from phylogenetics on Indo-European phonetic data in order to model language evolution. Heeringa and Joseph (2007) applied the Levensthein algorithm to the Dutch pronunciation data taken from *Reeks Nederlandse Dialectatlassen* and tried to reconstruct a 'proto-language' of Dutch dialects using the pairwise alignments.

Studies in historical linguistics and dialectometry where string comparison is used as a basis for calculating the distances between language varieties will profit from tools to multi-align strings automatically and to calculate the distances between them. Good multiple alignment is of benefit to all those methods in diachronic linguistics such as the comparative reconstruction method or the so-called CHARACTER-BASED METHODS taken from phylogenetics, which have also been successfully applied in linguistics (Gray and Jordan, 2000; Gray and Atkinson, 2003; Atkinson et al., 2005; Warnow et al., 2006). The multi-alignment systems can help historical linguistics by reducing the human labor needed to detect the regular sound correspondences and cognate pairs of words. They also systematize the linguistic knowledge in intuitive alignments, and provide a basis for the application of the quantitative methods that lead to a better understanding of language variation and language change.

In this study we apply an iterative pairwise alignment program for linguistics, ALPHAMALIG, on phonetic transcriptions of words used in dialectological research. We automatically multi-align all transcriptions and compare these generated alignments with manually aligned gold standard alignments. At the same time we propose two methods for the evaluation of the multiple sequence alignments (MSA).

The structure of this paper is as follows. An example of a multiple alignment and a discussion of the advantages over pairwise alignment is given in the next section, after which we discuss our data set in section 3. Section 4 explains the iterative pairwise alignment algorithm and the program ALPHAMALIG. Section 5 discusses the gold standard and two baselines, while section 6 discusses the novel evaluation procedures. The results are given in section 7 and we end this paper with a discussion in section 8.

2 Example of Multiple Sequence Alignment

In this section we will give an example of the automatically multi-aligned strings from our data set and point out some important features of the simultaneous comparison of more than two strings.

village1	j	ˈɑ	-	-	-	-
village2	j	ˈɑ	z	e	-	-
village3	-	ˈɑ	s	-	-	-
village4	j	ˈɑ	s	-	-	-
village5	j	ˈɑ	z	e	k	a
village6	j	ˈɛ	-	-	-	-
village7	-	ˈɒ	s	-	-	-

Figure 1: Example of multiple string alignment

In Figure 1 we have multi-aligned pronunciations of the word *az* 'I' automatically generated by ALPHAMALIG. The advantages of this kind of alignment over pairwise alignment are twofold:

- First, it is easier to detect and process corresponding phones in words and their alternations (like [ˈɑ] and [ˈɛ] and [ˈɒ] in the second column in Figure 1).
- Second, the distances/similarities between strings can be different in pairwise comparison as opposed to multiple comparison. This is so because multi-aligned strings, unlike pairwise aligned strings, contain information on the positions where phones were inserted or deleted in both strings. For example, in Figure 1 the pairwise alignment of the pronunciations from village 1 and village 3 would be:

village1	j	ˈɑ	-
village3	-	ˈɑ	s

These two alignments have one matching element out of three in total, which means that the similarity between them is $1/3 = 0.33$. At the same time the similarity between these two strings calculated based on the multi-aligned strings in Figure 1 would be $4/6 = 0.66$. The measurement based on multi-alignment takes the common missing material into account as well.

3 Data set

The data set used in this paper consists of phonetic transcriptions of 152 words collected from 197 sites evenly distributed all over Bulgaria. It is part of the project *Buldialect—Measuring linguistic unity and diversity in Europe*.[1] Pronunciations of almost all words were collected from all the sites and for some words there are multiple pronunciations per site. Phonetic transcriptions include various diacritics and suprasegmentals, making the total number of unique characters (types) in the data set 98.[2]

4 Iterative pairwise alignment

Multiple alignment algorithms iteratively merge two multiple alignments of two subsets of strings into a single multiple alignment that is union of those subsets (Gusfield, 1997). The simplest approach is to align the two strings that have the minimum distance over all pairs of strings and iteratively align strings having the smallest distance to the already aligned strings in order to generate a new multiple alignment. Other algorithms use different initializations and different criteria in selecting the new alignments to merge. Some begin with the longest (low cost) alignment instead of the least cost absolutely. A string with the smallest edit distance to any of the already merged strings is chosen to be added to the strings in the multiple alignment. In choosing the pair with the minimal distance, all algorithms are greedy, and risk missing optimal alignments.

ALPHAMALIG is an iterative pairwise alignment program for bilingual text alignment. It uses the strategy of merging multiple alignments of subsets of strings, instead of adding just one string at the time to the already aligned strings.[3] It was originally developed to align corresponding words in bilingual texts, i.e. with textual data, but it functions with any data that can be represented as a sequence of symbols of a finite alphabet. In addition to the input sequences, the program needs to know the alphabet and the distances between each token pair and each pair consisting of a token and a gap.

In order to perform multiple sequence alignments of X-SAMPA word transcriptions we modified ALPHAMALIG slightly so it could work with the tokens that consist of more than one symbol, such as ["e], ["e:] and [t_S]. The distances between the tokens were specified in such a way that vowels can be aligned only with vowels and consonants only with consonants. The same tokens are treated as identical and the distance between them is set to 0. The distance between any token in the data set to a gap symbol has the same cost as replacing a vowel with a vowel or a consonant with a consonant. Except for this very general linguistic knowledge, no other data-specific information was given to the program. In this research we do not use any phonetic features in order to define the segments more precisely and to calculate the distances between them in a more sensitive way than just making a binary 'match/does-not-match-distinction', since we want to keep the system language independent and robust to the highest possible degree.

5 Gold standard and baseline

In order to evaluate the performance of ALPHAMALIG, we compared the alignments obtained using this program to the manually aligned strings, our gold standard, and to the alignments obtained using two very simple techniques that are described next: simple baseline and advanced baseline.

5.1 Simple baseline

The simplest way of aligning two strings would be to align the first element from one string with the first element from the other string, the second element with the second and so on. If two strings are not of equal length, the remaining unaligned tokens are aligned with the gap symbol which rep-

[1]The project is sponsored by Volkswagen Stiftung. More information can be found at http://sfs.uni-tuebingen.de/dialectometry.

[2]The data is publicly available and can be found at http://www.bultreebank.org/BulDialects/index.html.

[3]More information on ALPHAMALIG can be found at http://alggen.lsi.upc.es/recerca/align/alphamalig/intro-alphamalig.html.

resents an insertion or a deletion. This is the alignment implicit in Hamming distance, which ignores insertions and deletions.

By applying this simple method, we obtained multiple sequence alignments for all words in our data set. An example of such a multiple sequence alignment is shown in Figure 2. These alignments were used to check how difficult the multiple sequence alignment task is for our data and how much improvement is obtained using more advanced techniques to multi-align strings.

j	ˈɑ	-	-
j	ˈɑ	z	e
ˈɑ	ʃ	-	-

Figure 2: Simple baseline

5.2 Advanced baseline

Our second baseline is more advanced than the first and was created using the following procedure:

1. for each word the longest string among all pronunciations is located
2. all strings are pairwise aligned against the longest string using the Levensthein algorithm (Heeringa, 2004). We refer to both sequences in a pairwise alignment as ALIGNMENT LINES. Note that alignment lines include hyphens indicating the places of insertions and deletions.
3. the alignment lines—all of equal length—are extracted
4. all extracted alignment lines are placed below each other to form the multiple alignment

An example of combining pairwise alignments against the longest string (in this case [jˈaze]) is shown in Figure 3.

5.3 Gold standard

Our gold standard was created by manually correcting the advanced baseline alignments described in the previous section. The gold standard results and both baseline results consist of 152 files with multi-aligned strings, one for each word. The pronunciations are ordered alphabetically according to the village they come from. If there are more pronunciations per site, they are all present, one under the other.

j	ˈɑ	z	e
j	ˈɑ	-	-

j	ˈɑ	z	e
-	ˈɑ	ʃ	-

j	ˈɑ	-	-
j	ˈɑ	z	e
-	ˈɑ	ʃ	-

Figure 3: Advanced baseline. The top two alignments each contain two alignment lines, and the bottom one contains three.

6 Evaluation

Although multiple sequence alignments are broadly used in molecular biology, there is still no widely accepted objective function for evaluating the goodness of the multiple aligned strings (Gusfield, 1997). The quality of the existing methods used to produce multiple sequence alignments is judged by the 'biological meaning of the alignments they produce'. Since strings in linguistics cannot be judged by the biological criteria used in string evaluation in biology, we were forced to propose evaluation methods that would be suitable for the strings in question. One of the advantages we had was the existence of the gold standard alignments, which made our task easier and more straightforward—in order to determine the quality of the multi-aligned strings, we compare outputs of the different algorithms to the gold standard. Since there is no off-the-shelf method that can be used for comparison of multi-aligned strings to a gold standard, we propose two novel methods—one sensitive to the order of columns in two alignments and another that takes into account only the content of each column.

6.1 Column dependent method

The first method we developed compares the contents of the columns and also takes the column sequence into account. The column dependent evaluation (CDE) procedure is as follows:

- Each gold standard column is compared to the most similar column out of two neighboring columns of a candidate multiple alignment. The two neighboring columns depend on the previous matched column j and have indices $j+1$ and $j+2$ (at the start $j=0$). It is possible that there are columns in the candidate multiple alignment which remain unmatched, as well as columns at the end of the gold standard which remain unmatched.

- The similarity of a candidate column with a gold standard column is calculated by dividing the number of correctly placed elements in every candidate column by the total number of elements in the column. A score of 1 indicates perfect overlap, while a score of 0 indicates the columns have no elements in common.

- The similarity score of the whole multiple alignment (for a single word) is calculated by summing the similarity score of each candidate column and dividing it by the total number of matched columns plus the total number of unmatched columns in both multiple alignments.

- The final similarity score between the set of gold standard alignments with the set of candidate multiple alignments is calculated by averaging the multiple alignment similarity scores for all strings.

As an example consider the multiple alignments in Figure 4, with the gold standard alignment (GS) on the left and the generated alignment (GA) on the right.

w	rʲ	'ɛ	m	e
v	r	'e	m	i
u	rʲ	'e	m	i
v	rʲ	'e	m	i

w	-	rʲ	'ɛ	m	e
v	-	r	'e	m	i
-	u	rʲ	'e	m	i
v	-	rʲ	'e	m	i

Figure 4: GS and ALPHAMALIG multiple string alignments, the gold standard alignment left, the ALPHAMALIG output right.

The evaluation starts by comparing the first column of the GS with the first and second column of the GA. The first column of the GA is the best match, since the similarity score between the first columns is 0.75 (3 out of 4 elements match). In similar fashion, the second column of the GS is compared with the second and the third column of the GA and matched with the third column of GA with a similarity score of 1 (all elements match). The third GS column is matched with the fourth GA column, the fourth GS column with the fifth GA column and the fifth GS column with the sixth GA column (all three having a similarity score of 1). As a consequence, the second column of the GA remains unmatched. In total, five columns are matched and one column remains unmatched. The total score of the GA equals:

$$\frac{(0.75 + 1 + 1 + 1 + 1)}{(5 + 1)} = 0.792$$

It is clear that this method punishes unmatched columns by increasing the value of the denominator in the similarity score calculation. As a consequence, swapped columns are punished severely, which is illustrated in Figure 5.

'o	rʲ	ə	j	-
'o	rʲ	ə	-	u
'o	rʲ	ə	f	-

'o	rʲ	ə	-	j
'o	rʲ	ə	u	-
'o	rʲ	ə	-	f

Figure 5: Two alignments with swapped columns

In the alignments in Figure 5, the first three columns of GS would be matched with the first three columns of GA with a score of 1, the fourth would be matched with the fifth, and two columns would be left unmatched: the fifth GS column and the fourth GA column yielding a total similarity score of $4/6 = 0.66$. Especially in this case this is undesirable, as both sequences of these columns represent equally reasonable multiple alignment and should have a total similarity score of 1. We therefore need a less strict evaluation method which does not insist on the exact ordering. An alternative method is introduced and discussed in the following section.

6.2 Modified Rand Index

In developing an alternative evaluation we proceeded from the insight that the columns of a multiple alignment are a sort of PARTITION of the elements of the alignment strings, i.e., they constitute a set of disjoint multi-sets whose union is the entire multi-set of segments in the multiple alignment. Each column effectively assigns its segments to a partition, which clearly cannot overlap with the elements of another column (partition). Since every segment must fall within some column, the assignment is also exhaustive.

Our second evaluation method is therefore based on the modified Rand index (Hubert and Arabie, 1985). The modified Rand index is used in classification for comparing two different partitions of a finite set of objects. It is based on the Rand index (Rand, 1971), one of the most popular measures for comparing the degree to which partitions agree (in classification).

Given a set of n elements $S = o_1, ...o_n$ and two partitions of S, U and V, the Rand index R is defined as:

$$R = \frac{a+b}{a+b+c+d}$$

where:

- a: the number of pairs of elements in S that are in the same set (column) in U and in the same set in V
- b: the number of pairs of elements in S that are in different sets (columns) in U and in different sets in V
- c: the number of pairs of elements in S that are in the same set in U and in different sets in V
- d: the number of pairs of elements in S that are in different sets in U and in the same set in V

Consequently, a and b are the number of pairs of elements on which two classifications agree, while c and d are the number of pairs of elements on which they disagree. In our case classifications agree about concrete segment tokens only in the cases where they appear in the same columns in the alignments.

The value of Rand index ranges between 0 and 1, with 0 indicating that the two partitions (multi-alignments) do not agree on any pair of points and 1 indicating that the data partitions are exactly the same.[4] A problem with the Rand index is that it does not return a constant value (zero) if two partitions are picked at random. Hubert and Arabie (1985) suggested a modification of the Rand index (MRI) that corrects this property. It can be expressed in the general form as:

$$\text{MRI} = \frac{\text{Rand index} - \text{Expected index}}{\text{Maximum index} - \text{Expected index}}$$

The expected index is the expected number of pairs which would be placed in the same set in U and in the same set in V by chance. The maximum index represents the maximum number of objects that can be put in the same set in U and in the same set in V. The MRI value ranges between -1 and 1, with perfect overlap being indicated by 1 and values ≤ 0 indicating no overlap. For a more detailed explanation of the modified Rand index, please refer to Hubert and Arabie (1985).

[4]In dialectometry, this index was used by Heeringa et al. (2002) to validate dialect clustering methods.

We would like to emphasize that it is clear that the set of columns of a multi-alignment have more structure than a partition *sec*, in particular because the columns (subpartitions) are ordered, unlike the subpartitions in a partition. But we shall compensate for this difference by explicitly marking order.

ˈo [1]	rʲ [2]	ə [3]	j [4]	-
ˈo [5]	rʲ [6]	ə [7]	-	u [8]
ˈo [9]	rʲ [10]	ə [11]	f [12]	-

Figure 6: Annotated alignment

In our study, each segment token in each transcription was treated as a different object (see Figure 6), and every column was taken to be a subpartition to which segment tokens are assigned. Both alignments in Figure 5 have 12 phones that are put into 5 groups. We "tag" each token sequentially in order to distinguish the different tokens of a single segment from each other, but note that the way we do this also introduces an order sensitivity in the measure. The two partitions obtained are:

GS1 = {1,5,9}	GA1 = {1,5,9}
GS2 = {2,6,10}	GA2 = {2,6,10}
GS3 = {3,7,11}	GA3 = {3,7,11}
GS4 = {4,12}	GA4 = {8}
GS5 = {8}	GA5 = {4,12}

Using the modified Rand index the quality of each column is checked, regardless of whether the columns are in order. The MRI for the alignments in Figure 5 will be 1, because both alignments group segment tokens in the same way. Even though columns four and five are swapped, in both classifications phones [j] and [f] are grouped together, while sound [u] forms a separate group.

The MRI itself only takes into account the quality of each column separately since it simply checks whether the same elements are together in the candidate alignment as in the gold-standard alignment. It is therefore insensitive to the ordering of columns. While it may have seemed counterintuitive linguistically to proceed from an order-insensitive measure, the comparison of "tagged tokens" described above effectively reintroduces order sensitivity.

In the next section we describe the results of applying both evaluation methods on the automatically generated multiple alignments.

7 Results

After comparing all files of the baseline algorithms and ALPHAMALIG against the gold standard files according to the column dependent evaluation method and the modified Rand index, the average score is calculated by summing up all scores and dividing them by the number of word files (152).

The results are given in Table 1 and also include the number of words with perfect multi-alignments (i.e. identical to the gold standard). Using CDE, ALPHAMALIG scored 0.932 out of 1.0 with 103 perfectly aligned files. The result for the simple baseline was 0.710 with 44 perfectly aligned files. As expected, the result for the advanced baseline was in between these two results—0.869 with 72 files that were completely identical to the GS files. Using MRI to evaluate the alignments generated we obtained generally higher scores for all three algorithms, but with the same ordering. ALPHAMALIG scored 0.982, with 104 perfectly aligned files. The advanced baseline had a lower score of 0.937 and 74 perfect alignments. The simple baseline performed worse, scoring 0.848 and having 44 perfectly aligned files.

The scores of the CDE evaluation method are lower than the MRI scores, which is due to the first method's problematic sensitivity to column ordering in the alignments. It is clear that in both evaluation methods ALPHAMALIG outperforms both baseline alignments by a wide margin.

It is important to notice that the scores for the simple baseline are reasonably high, which can be explained by the structure of our data set. The variation of word pronunciations is relatively small, making string alignment easier. However, ALPHAMALIG obtained much higher scores using both evaluation methods.

Additional qualitative error analysis reveals that the errors of ALPHAMALIG are mostly caused by the vowel-vowel consonant-consonant alignment restriction. In the data set there are 21 files that contain metathesis. Since vowel-consonant alignments were not allowed in ALPHAMALIG, alignments produced by this algorithm were different from the gold standard, as illustrated in Figure 7.

The vowel-consonant restriction is also responsible for wrong alignments in some words where metathesis is not present, but where the vowel-consonant alignment is still preferred over aligning vowels and/or consonants with a gap (see for example Figure 4).

v	l	'ɤ	k		v	l	'ɤ	-	k
v	'ɤ	l	k		v	-	'ɤ	l	k

Figure 7: Two alignments with metathesis

The other type of error present in the ALPHAMALIG alignments is caused by the fact that all vowel-vowel and consonant-consonant distances receive the same weight. In Figure 8 the alignment of word *bjahme* 'were' produced by ALPHAMALIG is wrong because instead of aligning [mʲ] with [m] and [m] it is wrongly aligned with [x] and [x], while [x] is aligned with [ʃ] instead of aligning it with [x] and [x].

b	'ɛ	**ʃ**	u	**x**	-	m	e	-
bʲ	'ɑ	**-**	-	**x**	-	m	i	-
b	'e	**x**	-	**mʲ**	-	-	ɤ	-

Figure 8: Alignment error produced by ALPHAMALIG

8 Discussion and future work

In this study we presented a first attempt to automatically multi-align phonetic transcriptions. The algorithm we used to generate alignments has been shown to be very reliable, produce alignments of good quality, with less than 2% error at the segment level. In this study we used only very simple linguistic knowledge in order to align strings. The only restriction we imposed was that a vowel should only be aligned with a vowel and a consonant only with a consonant. The system has shown to be very robust and to produce good quality alignments with a very limited information on the distances between the tokens. However, in the future we would like to apply this algorithm using more detailed segment distances, so that we can work without vowel-consonant restrictions. Using more detailed language specific feature system for each phone, we believe we may be able to improve the produced alignments further. This especially holds for the type of errors illustrated in Figure 8 where it is clear that [mʲ] is phonetically closer to [m] than to [x] sound.

As our data set was relatively simple (indicated by the reasonable performance of our simple baseline algorithm), we would very much like to evaluate ALPHAMALIG against a more complex data

	CDE	CDE perfect columns	MRI	MRI perfect columns
Simple baseline	0.710	44	0.848	44
Advanced baseline	0.869	72	0.937	74
ALPHAMALIG	**0.932**	**103**	**0.982**	**104**

Table 1: Results of evaluating outputs of the different algorithms against the GS

set and try to replicate the good results we obtained here. On one hand, high performance of both baseline algorithms show that our task was relatively easy. On the other hand, achieving perfect alignments will be very difficult, if possible at all.

Additionally, we proposed two methods to evaluate multiple aligned strings in linguistic research. Although these systems could be improved, both of them are giving a good estimation of the quality of the generated alignments. For the examined data, we find MRI to be better evaluation technique since it overcomes the problem of swapped columns.

In this research we tested and evaluated ALPHAMALIG on the dialect phonetic data. However, multiple sequence alignments can be also applied on the sequences of sentences and paragraphs. This makes multiple sequence alignment algorithm a powerful tool for mining text data in social sciences, humanities and education.

Acknowledgements

We are thankful to Xavier Messeguer of the Technical University of Catalonia who kindly supplied us with the source code of ALPHAMALIG. We also thank Therese Leinonen and Sebastian Kürschner of the University of Groningen and Esteve Valls i Alecha of the University of Barcelona for their useful feedback on our ideas.

References

Laura Alonso, Irene Castellon, Jordi Escribano, Xavier Messeguer, and Lluis Padro. 2004. Multiple Sequence Alignment for characterizing the linear structure of revision. In *Proceedings of the 4th International Conference on Language Resources and Evaluation*.

Quentin Atkinson, Geoff Nicholls, David Welch, and Russell Gray. 2005. From words to dates: water into wine, mathemagic or phylogenetic inference. *Transcriptions of the Philological Society*, 103:193–219.

Lyle Campbell. 2004. *Historical Linguistics: An Introduction*. Edinburgh University Press, second edition.

Russel D. Gray and Quentin D. Atkinson. 2003. Language-tree divergence times support the Anatolian theory of Indo-European origin. *Nature*, 426:435–339.

Russel D. Gray and Fiona M. Jordan. 2000. Language trees support the express-train sequence of Austronesian expansion. *Nature*, 405:1052–1055.

Dan Gusfield. 1997. *Algorithms on Strings, Trees and Sequences: Computer Science and Computational Biology*. Cambridge University Press.

Wilbert Heeringa and Brian Joseph. 2007. The relative divergence of Dutch dialect pronunciations from their common source: An exploratory study. In John Nerbonne, T. Mark Ellison, and Grzegorz Kondrak, editors, *Proceedings of the Ninth Meeting of the ACL Special Interest Group in Computational Morphology and Phonology*.

Wilbert Heeringa, John Nerbonne, and Peter Kleiweg. 2002. Validating dialect comparison methods. In Wolfgang Gaul and Gunter Ritter, editors, *Classification, Automation, and New Media. Proceedings of the 24th Annual Conference of the Gesellschaft für Klassifikation e. V., University of Passau, March 15-17, 2000*, pages 445–452. Springer, Berlin, Heidelberg and New York.

Wilbert Heeringa. 2004. *Measuring Dialect Pronunciation Differences using Levenshtein Distance*. Ph.D. thesis, Rijksuniversiteit Groningen.

Lawrence Hubert and Phipps Arabie. 1985. Comparing partitions. *Journal of Classification*, 2:193–218.

Grzegorz Kondrak. 2002. *Algorithms for Language Reconstruction*. PhD Thesis, University of Toronto.

William M. Rand. 1971. Objective criteria for the evaluation of clustering methods. *Journal of American Statistical Association*, 66(336):846–850, December.

Tandy Warnow, Steven N. Evans, Donald Ringe, and Luay Nakhleh. 2006. A stochastic model of language evolution that incorporates homoplasy and borrowing. In Peter Forster and Colin Renfrew, editors, *Phylogenetic Methods and the Prehistory of Languages*. MacDonald Institute for Archaeological Research, Cambridge.

Evaluating the pairwise string alignment of pronunciations

Martijn Wieling
University of Groningen
The Netherlands
m.b.wieling@rug.nl

Jelena Prokić
University of Groningen
The Netherlands
j.prokic@rug.nl

John Nerbonne
University of Groningen
The Netherlands
j.nerbonne@rug.nl

Abstract

Pairwise string alignment (PSA) is an important general technique for obtaining a measure of similarity between two strings, used e.g., in dialectology, historical linguistics, transliteration, and in evaluating name distinctiveness. The current study focuses on evaluating different PSA methods at the alignment level instead of via the distances it induces. About 3.5 million pairwise alignments of Bulgarian phonetic dialect data are used to compare four algorithms with a manually corrected gold standard. The algorithms evaluated include three variants of the Levenshtein algorithm as well as the Pair Hidden Markov Model. Our results show that while all algorithms perform very well and align around 95% of all alignments correctly, there are specific qualitative differences in the (mis)alignments of the different algorithms.

1 Introduction

Our cultural heritage is not only accessible through museums, libraries, archives and their digital portals, it is alive and well in the varied cultural habits practiced today by the various peoples of the world. To research and understand this cultural heritage we require instruments which are sensitive to its signals, and, in particular sensitive to signals of common provenance. The present paper focuses on speech habits which even today bear signals of common provenance in the various dialects of the world's languages, and which have also been recorded and preserved in major archives of folk culture internationally. We present work in a research line which seeks to develop digital instruments capable of detecting common provenance among pronunciation habits, focusing in this paper on the issue of evaluating the quality of these instruments.

Pairwise string alignment (PSA) methods, like the popular Levenshtein algorithm (Levenshtein, 1965) which uses insertions (alignments of a segment against a gap), deletions (alignments of a gap against a segment) and substitutions (alignments of two segments) often form the basis of determining the distance between two strings. Since there are many alignment algorithms and specific settings for each algorithm influencing the distance between two strings (Nerbonne and Kleiweg, 2007), evaluation is very important in determining the effectiveness of the distance methods.

Determining the distance (or similarity) between two phonetic strings is an important aspect of dialectometry, and alignment quality is important in applications in which string alignment is a goal in itself, for example, determining if two words are likely to be cognate (Kondrak, 2003), detecting confusable drug names (Kondrak and Dorr, 2003), or determining whether a string is the transliteration of the same name from another writing system (Pouliquen, 2008).

In this paper we evaluate string distance measures on the basis of data from dialectology. We therefore explain a bit more of the intended use of the pronunciation distance measure.

Dialect atlases normally contain a large number of pronunciations of the same word in various places throughout a language area. All pairs of pronunciations of corresponding words are compared in order to obtain a measure of the aggregate linguistic distance between dialectal varieties (Heeringa, 2004). It is clear that the quality of the measurement is of crucial importance.

Almost all evaluation methods in dialectometry focus on the aggregate results and ignore the individual word-pair distances and individual alignments on which the distances are based. The focus on the aggregate distance of 100 or so word

Proceedings of the EACL 2009 Workshop on Language Technology and Resources for Cultural Heritage, Social Sciences, Humanities, and Education –LaTeCH – SHELT&R 2009, pages 26–34,
Athens, Greece, 30 March 2009.

pairs effectively hides many differences between methods. For example, Heeringa et al. (2006) find no significant differences in the degrees to which several pairwise string distance measures correlate with perceptual distances when examined at an aggregate level. Wieling et al. (2007) and Wieling and Nerbonne (2007) also report almost no difference between different PSA algorithms at the aggregate level. It is important to be able to evaluate the different techniques more sensitively, which is why this paper examines alignment quality at the segment level.

Kondrak (2003) applies a PSA algorithm to align words in different languages in order to detect cognates automatically. Exceptionally, he does provide an evaluation of the string alignments generated by different algorithms. But he restricts his examination to a set of only 82 gold standard pairwise alignments and he only distinguishes correct and incorrect alignments and does not look at misaligned phones.

In the current study we introduce and evaluate several alignment algorithms more extensively at the alignment level. The algorithms we evaluate include the Levenshtein algorithm (with syllabicity constraint), which is one of the most popular alignment methods and has successfully been used in determining pronunciation differences in phonetic strings (Kessler, 1995; Heeringa, 2004). In addition we look at two adaptations of the Levenshtein algorithm. The first adaptation includes the swap-operation (Wagner and Lowrance, 1975), while the second adaptation includes phonetic segment distances, which are generated by applying an iterative pointwise mutual information (PMI) procedure (Church and Hanks, 1990). Finally we include alignments generated with the Pair Hidden Markov Model (PHMM) as introduced to language studies by Mackay and Kondrak (2005). They reported that the Pair Hidden Markov Model outperformed ALINE, the best performing algorithm at the alignment level in the aforementioned study of Kondrak (2003). The PHMM has also successfully been used in dialectology by Wieling et al. (2007).

2 Dataset

The dataset used in this study consists of 152 words collected from 197 sites equally distributed over Bulgaria. The transcribed word pronunciations include diacritics and suprasegmentals (e.g., intonation). The total number of different phonetic types (or segments) is 98.[1]

The gold standard pairwise alignment was automatically generated from a manually corrected gold standard set of N multiple alignments (see Prokić et al., 2009) in the following way:

- Every individual string (including gaps) in the multiple alignment is aligned with every other string of the same word. With 152 words and 197 sites and in some cases more than one pronunciations per site for a certain word, the total number of pairwise alignments is about 3.5 million.

- If a resulting pairwise alignment contains a gap in both strings at the same position (a gap-gap alignment), these gaps are removed from the pairwise alignment. We justify this, reasoning that no alignment algorithm may be expected to detect parallel deletions in a single pair of words. There is no evidence for this in the single pair.

To make this clear, consider the multiple alignment of three Bulgarian dialectal variants of the word 'I' (as in 'I am'):

j	ˈɑ	s	
	ˈɑ	z	i
j	ˈɑ		

Using the procedure above, the three generated pairwise alignments are:

j	ˈɑ	s		j	ˈɑ	s		ˈɑ	z	i
	ˈɑ	z	i	j	ˈɑ		j	ˈɑ		

3 Algorithms

Four algorithms are evaluated with respect to the quality of their alignments, including three variants of the Levenshtein algorithm and the Pair Hidden Markov Model.

3.1 The VC-sensitive Levenshtein algorithm

The Levenshtein algorithm is a very efficient dynamic programming algorithm, which was first introduced by Kessler (1995) as a tool for computationally comparing dialects. The Levenshtein distance between two strings is determined by counting the minimum number of edit operations (i.e. insertions, deletions and substitutions) needed to transform one string into the other.

[1]The dataset is available online at the website http://www.bultreebank.org/BulDialects/

For example, the Levenshtein distance between [j'ɑs] and ['ɑzi], two Bulgarian dialectal variants of the word 'I' (as in 'I am'), is 3:

j'ɑs	delete j	1
'ɑs	subst. s/z	1
'ɑz	insert i	1
'ɑzi		
		3

The corresponding alignment is:

j	'ɑ	s	
	'ɑ	z	i
1		1	1

The Levenshtein distance has been used frequently and successfully in measuring linguistic distances in several languages, including Irish (Kessler, 1995), Dutch (Heeringa, 2004) and Norwegian (Heeringa, 2004). Additionally, the Levenshtein distance has been shown to yield aggregate results that are consistent (Cronbach's $\alpha = 0.99$) and valid when compared to dialect speakers judgements of similarity ($r \approx 0.7$; Heeringa et al., 2006).

Following Heeringa (2004), we have adapted the Levenshtein algorithm slightly, so that it does not allow alignments of vowels with consonants. We refer to this adapted algorithm as the VC-sensitive Levenshtein algorithm.

3.2 The Levenshtein algorithm with the swap operation

Because metathesis (i.e. transposition of sounds) occurs relatively frequently in the Bulgarian dialect data (in 21 of 152 words), we extend the VC-sensitive Levenshtein algorithm as described in section 3.1 to include the swap-operation (Wagner and Lowrance, 1975), which allows two adjacent characters to be interchanged. The swap-operation is also known as a transposition, which was introduced with respect to detecting spelling errors by Damerau (1964). As a consequence the Damerau distance refers to the minimum number of insertions, deletions, substitutions and transpositions required to transform one string into the other. In contrast to Wagner and Lowrance (1975) and in line with Damerau (1964) we restrict the swap operation to be only allowed for string X and Y when $x_i = y_{i+1}$ and $y_i = x_{i+1}$ (with x_i being the token at position i in string X):

x_i	x_{i+1}
y_i	y_{i+1}
><	1

Note that a swap-operation in the alignment is indicated by the symbol '><'. The first number following this symbol indicates the cost of the swap-operation.

Consider the alignment of [vr'ɤ] and [v'ɤr],[2] two Bulgarian dialectal variants of the word 'peak' (mountain). The alignment involves a swap and results in a total Levenshtein distance of 1:

v	r	'ɤ
v	'ɤ	r
	><	1

However, the alignment of the transcription [vr'ɤ] with another dialectal transcription [v'ar] does not allow a swap and yields a total Levenshtein distance of 2:

v		r	'ɤ
v	'a	r	
	1		1

Including just the option of swapping identical segments in the implementation of the Levenshtein algorithm is relatively easy. We set the cost of the swap operation to one[3] plus twice the cost of substituting x_i with y_{i+1} plus twice the cost of substituting y_i with x_{i+1}. In this way the swap operation will be preferred when $x_i = y_{i+1}$ and $y_i = x_{i+1}$, but not when $x_i \neq y_{i+1}$ and/or $y_i \neq x_{i+1}$. In the first case the cost of the swap operation is 1, which is less than the cost of the alternative of two substitutions. In the second case the cost is either 3 (if $x_i \neq y_{i+1}$ or $y_i \neq x_{i+1}$) or 5 (if $x_i \neq y_{i+1}$ and $y_i \neq x_{i+1}$), which is higher than the cost of using insertions, deletions and/or substitutions.

Just as in the previous section, we do not allow vowels to align with consonants (except in the case of a swap).

3.3 The Levenshtein algorithm with generated segment distances

The VC-sensitive Levenshtein algorithm as described in section 3.1 only distinguishes between vowels and consonants. However, more sensitive segment distances are also possible. Heeringa (2004) experimented with specifying phonetic segment distances based on phonetic features and

[2]We use transcriptions in which stress is marked on stressed vowels instead of before stressed syllables. We follow in this the Bulgarian convention instead of the IPA convention.

[3]Actually the cost is set to 0.999 to prefer an alignment involving a swap over an alternative alignment involving only regular edit operations.

also based on acoustic differences derived from spectrograms, but he did not obtain improved results at the aggregate level.

Instead of using segment distances as these are (incompletely) suggested by phonetic or phonological theory, we tried to determine the sound distances automatically based on the available data. We used pointwise mutual information (PMI; Church and Hanks, 1990) to obtain these distances. It generates segment distances by assessing the degree of statistical dependence between the segments x and y:

$$\text{PMI}(x, y) = \log_2 \left(\frac{p(x, y)}{p(x)\, p(y)} \right) \quad (1)$$

Where:

- $p(x, y)$: the number of times x and y occur at the same position in two aligned strings X and Y, divided by the total number of aligned segments (i.e. the relative occurrence of the aligned segments x and y in the whole dataset). Note that either x or y can be a gap in the case of insertion or deletion.

- $p(x)$ and $p(y)$: the number of times x (or y) occurs, divided by the total number of segment occurrences (i.e. the relative occurrence of x or y in the whole dataset). Dividing by this term normalizes the empirical frequency with respect to the frequency expected if x and y are statistically independent.

The greater the PMI value, the more segments tend to cooccur in correspondences. Negative PMI values indicate that segments do not tend to cooccur in correspondences, while positive PMI values indicate that segments tend to cooccur in correspondences. The segment distances can therefore be generated by subtracting the PMI value from 0 and adding the maximum PMI value (i.e. lowest distance is 0). In that way corresponding segments obtain the lowest distance.

Based on the PMI value and its conversion to segment distances, we developed an iterative procedure to automatically obtain the segment distances:

1. The string alignments are generated using the VC-sensitive Levenshtein algorithm (see section 3.1).[4]

2. The PMI value for every segment pair is calculated according to (1) and subsequently transformed to a segment distance by subtracting it from zero and adding the maximum PMI value.

3. The Levenshtein algorithm using these segment distances is applied to generate a new set of alignments.

4. Step 2 and 3 are repeated until the alignments of two consecutive iterations do not differ (i.e. convergence is reached).

The potential merit of using PMI-generated segment distances can be made clear by the following example. Consider the strings [vˈɤn] and [vˈɤɳkə], Bulgarian dialectal variants of the word 'outside'. The VC-sensitive Levenshtein algorithm yields the following (correct) alignment:

v	ˈɤ	n		
v	ˈɤ	ɳ	k	ə
		1	1	1

But also the alternative (incorrect) alignment:

v	ˈɤ		n	
v	ˈɤ	ɳ	k	ə
		1	1	1

The VC-sensitive Levenshtein algorithm generates the erroneous alignment because it has no way to identify that the consonant [n] is nearer to the consonant [ɳ] than to the consonant [k]. In contrast, the Levenshtein algorithm which uses the PMI-generated segment distances only generates the correct first alignment, because the [n] occurs relatively more often aligned with [ɳ] than with [k] so that the distance between [n] and [ɳ] will be lower than the distance between [n] and [k]. The idea behind this procedure is similar to Ristad's suggestion to learn segment distances for edit distance using an expectation maximization algorithm (Ristad and Yianilos, 1998). Our approach differs from their approach in that we only learn segment distances based on the alignments generated by the VC-sensitive Levenshtein algorithm, while Ristad and Yianilos (1998) learn segment distances by considering all possible alignments of two strings.

3.4 The Pair Hidden Markov Model

The Pair Hidden Markov Model (PHMM) also generates alignments based on automatically generated segment distances and has been used suc-

[4]We also used the Levenshtein algorithm without the vowel-consonant restriction to generate the PMI values, but this had a negative effect on the performance.

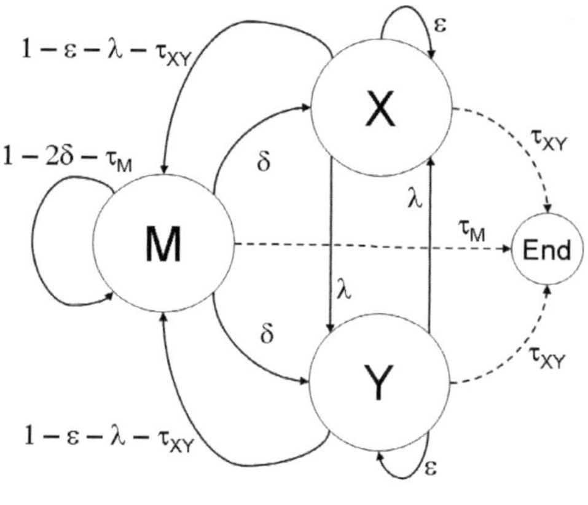

Figure 1: Pair Hidden Markov Model. Image courtesy of Mackay and Kondrak (2005).

cessfully in language studies (Mackay and Kondrak, 2005; Wieling et al., 2007).

A Hidden Markov Model (HMM) is a probabilistic finite-state transducer that generates an observation sequence by starting in an initial state, going from state to state based on transition probabilities and emitting an output symbol in each state based on the emission probabilities in that state for that output symbol (Rabiner, 1989). The PHMM was originally proposed by Durbin et al. (1998) for aligning biological sequences and was first used in linguistics by Mackay and Kondrak (2005) to identify cognates. The PHMM differs from the regular HMM in that it outputs two observation streams (i.e. a series of alignments of pairs of individual segments) instead of only a series of single symbols. The PHMM displayed in Figure 1 has three emitting states: the substitution ('match') state (M) which emits two aligned symbols, the insertion state (Y) which emits a symbol and a gap, and the deletion state (X) which emits a gap and a symbol.

The following example shows the state sequence for the pronunciations [jˈɑs] and [ˈɑzi] (English 'I'):

j	ˈɑ	s	
	ˈɑ	z	i
X	M	M	Y

Before generating the alignments, all probabilities of the PHMM have to be estimated. These probabilities consist of the 5 transition probabilities shown in Figure 1: ϵ, λ, δ, τ_{XY} and τ_M. In addition there are 98 emission probabilities for the insertion state and the deletion state (one for every segment) and 9604 emission probabilities for the substitution state. The probability of starting in one of the three states is set equal to the probability of going from the substitution state to that particular state. The Baum-Welch expectation maximization algorithm (Baum et al., 1970) can be used to iteratively reestimate these probabilities until a local optimum is found.

To prevent order effects in training, every word pair is considered twice (e.g., $w_a - w_b$ and $w_b - w_a$). The resulting insertion and deletion probabilities are therefore the same (for each segment), and the probability of substituting x for y is equal to the probability of substituting y for x, effectively yielding 4802 distinct substitution probabilities.

Wieling et al. (2007) showed that using Dutch dialect data for training, sensible segment distances were obtained; acoustic vowel distances on the basis of spectrograms correlated significantly ($r = -0.72$) with the vowel substitution probabilities of the PHMM. Additionally, probabilities of substituting a symbol with itself were much higher than the probabilities of substituting an arbitrary vowel with another non-identical vowel (*mutatis mutandis* for consonants), which were in turn much higher than the probabilities of substituting a vowel for a consonant.

After training, the well known Viterbi algorithm can be used to obtain the best alignments (Rabiner, 1989).

4 Evaluation

As described in section 2, we use the generated pairwise alignments from a gold standard of multiple alignments for evaluation. In addition, we look at the performance of a baseline of pairwise alignments, which is constructed by aligning the strings according to the Hamming distance (i.e. only allowing substitutions and no insertions or deletions; Hamming, 1950).

The evaluation procedure consists of comparing the alignments of the previously discussed algorithms including the baseline with the alignments of the gold standard. For the comparison we use the standard Levenshtein algorithm without any restrictions. The evaluation proceeds as follows:

1. The pairwise alignments of the four algorithms, the baseline and the gold standard are generated and standardized (see section 4.1). When multiple equal-scoring alignments are

generated by an algorithm, only one (i.e. the final) alignment is selected.

2. In each alignment, we convert each pair of aligned segments to a single token, so that every alignment of two strings is converted to a single string of segment pairs.
3. For every algorithm these transformed strings are aligned with the transformed strings of the gold standard using the standard Levenshtein algorithm.
4. The Levenshtein distances for all these strings are summed up resulting in the total distance between every alignment algorithm and the gold standard. Only if individual segments match completely the segment distance is 0, otherwise it is 1.

To illustrate this procedure, consider the following gold standard alignment of [vlˈɤk] and [vˈɤlk], two Bulgarian dialectal variants of the word 'wolf':

v	l	ˈɤ	k
v	ˈɤ	l	k

Every aligned segment pair is converted to a single token by adding the symbol '/' between the segments and using the symbol '-' to indicate a gap. This yields the following transformed string:

v/v l/ˈɤ ˈɤ/l k/k

Suppose another algorithm generates the following alignment (not detecting the swap):

v	l	ˈɤ		k
v		ˈɤ	l	k

The transformed string for this alignment is:

v/v l/- ˈɤ/ˈɤ -/l k/k

To evaluate this alignment, we align this string to the transformed string of the gold standard and obtain a Levenshtein distance of 3:

v/v	l/ˈɤ	ˈɤ/l		k/k
v/v	l/-	ˈɤ/ˈɤ	-/l	k/k
	1	1	1	

By repeating this procedure for all alignments and summing up all distances, we obtain total distances between the gold standard and every alignment algorithm. Algorithms which generate high-quality alignments will have a low distance from the gold standard, while the distance will be higher for algorithms which generate low-quality alignments.

4.1 Standardization

The gold standard contains a number of alignments which have alternative equivalent alignments, most notably an alignment containing an insertion followed by a deletion (which is equal to the deletion followed by the insertion), or an alignment containing a syllabic consonant such as [ˈɹ̩], which in fact matches both a vowel and a neighboring r-like consonant and can therefore be aligned with either the vowel or the consonant. In order to prevent punishing the algorithms which do not match the exact gold standard in these cases, the alignments of the gold standard and all alignment algorithms are transformed to one standard form in all relevant cases.

For example, consider the correct alignment of [vˈiɑ] and [vˈij], two Bulgarian dialectal variations of the English plural pronoun 'you':

v	ˈi		ɑ
v	ˈi	j	

Of course, this alignment is as reasonable as:

v	ˈi	ɑ	
v	ˈi		j

To avoid punishing the first, we transform all insertions followed by deletions to deletions followed by insertions, effectively scoring the two alignments the same.

For the syllabic consonants we transform all alignments to a form in which the syllabic consonant is followed by a gap and not vice versa. For instance, aligning [vˈɹ̩x] with [vˈɑrx] (English: 'peak') yields:

v		ˈɹ̩	x
v	ˈɑ	r	x

Which is transformed to the equivalent alignment:

v	ˈɹ̩		x
v	ˈɑ	r	x

5 Results

We will report both quantitative results using the evaluation method discussed in the previous section, as well as the qualitative results, where we focus on characteristic errors of the different alignment algorithms.

5.1 Quantitative results

Because there are two algorithms which use generated segment distances (or probabilities) in their alignments, we first check if these values are sensible and comparable to each other.

5.1.1 Comparison of segment distances

With respect to the PMI results (convergence was reached after 7 iterations, taking less than 5 CPU minutes), we indeed found sensible results: the average distance between identical symbols was significantly lower than the distance between pairs of different vowels and consonants ($t < -13, p < .001$). Because we did not allow vowel-consonants alignments in the Levenshtein algorithm, no PMI values were generated for those segment pairs.

Just as Wieling et al. (2007), we found sensible PHMM substitution probabilities (convergence was reached after 1675 iterations, taking about 7 CPU hours): the probability of matching a symbol with itself was significantly higher than the probability of substituting one vowel for another (similarly for consonants), which in turn was higher than the probability of substituting a vowel with a consonant (all t's $> 9, p < .001$).

To allow a fair comparison between the PHMM probabilities and the PMI distances, we transformed the PHMM probabilities to log-odds scores (i.e. dividing the probability by the relative frequency of the segments and subsequently taking the log). Because the residues after the linear regression between the PHMM similarities and PMI distances were not normally distributed, we used Spearman's rank correlation coefficient to assess the relationship between the two variables. We found a highly significant Spearman's $\rho = -.965\,(p < .001)$, which means that the relationship between the PHMM similarities and the PMI distances is very strong. When looking at the insertions and deletions we also found a significant relationship: Spearman's $\rho = -.736\,(p < .001)$.

5.1.2 Evaluation against the gold standard

Using the procedure described in section 4, we calculated the distances between the gold standard and the alignment algorithms. Besides reporting the total number of misaligned tokens, we also divided this number by the total number of aligned segments in the gold standard (about 16 million) to get an idea of the error rate. Note that the error rate is 0 in the perfect case, but might rise to nearly 2 in the worst case, which is an alignment consisting of only insertions and deletions and therefore up to twice as long as the alignments in the gold standard. Finally, we also report the total number of alignments (word pairs) which are not exactly equal to the alignments of the gold standard.

The results are shown in Table 1. We can clearly see that all algorithms beat the baseline and align about 95% of all string pairs correctly. While the Levenshtein PMI algorithm aligns most strings perfectly, it misaligns slightly more individual segments than the PHMM and the Levenshtein algorithm with the swap operation (i.e. it makes more segment alignment errors per word pair). The VC-sensitive Levenshtein algorithm in general performs slightly worse than the other three algorithms.

5.2 Qualitative results

Let us first note that it is almost impossible for any algorithm to achieve a perfect overlap with the gold standard, because the gold standard was generated from multiple alignments and therefore incorporates other constraints. For example, while a certain pairwise alignment could appear correct in aligning two consonants, the multiple alignment could show contextual support (from pronunciations in other varieties) for separating the consonants. Consequently, all algorithms discussed below make errors of this kind.

In general, the specific errors of the VC-sensitive Levenshtein algorithm can be separated into three cases. First, as we illustrated in section 3.3, the VC-sensitive Levenshtein algorithm has no way to distinguish between aligning a consonant with one of two neighboring consonants and sometimes chooses the wrong one (this also holds for vowels). Second, it does not allow alignments of vowels with consonants and therefore cannot detect correct vowel-consonant alignments such as correspondences of [u] with [v] initially. Third, for the same reason the VC-sensitive Levenshtein algorithm is also not able to detect metathesis of vowels with consonants.

The misalignments of the Levenshtein algorithm with the swap-operation can also be split in three cases. It suffers from the same two problems as the VC-sensitive Levenshtein algorithm in choosing to align a consonant incorrectly with one of two neighboring consonants and not being able to align a vowel with a consonant. Third, even though it aligns some of the metathesis cases correctly, it also makes some errors by incorrectly applying the swap-operation. For example, consider the alignment of [sˈirʲɪni] and [sˈirʲnɪ], two Bulgarian dialectal variations of the word 'cheese', in which the swap-operation is applied:

Algorithm	Misaligned segments (error rate)	Incorrect alignments (%)
Baseline (Hamming algorithm)	2510094 (0.1579)	726844 (20.92%)
VC-sens. Levenshtein algorithm	490703 (0.0309)	191674 (5.52%)
Levenshtein PMI algorithm	399216 (0.0251)	**156440 (4.50%)**
Levenshtein swap algorithm	392345 (0.0247)	161834 (4.66%)
Pair Hidden Markov Model	**362423 (0.0228)**	160896 (4.63%)

Table 1: Comparison to gold standard alignments. All differences are significant ($p < 0.01$).

s	ˈi	rʲ	ɪ	n	i
s	ˈi	rʲ	n	ɪ	
0	0	0	><	1	1

However, the two ɪ's are not related and should not be swapped, which is reflected in the gold standard alignment:

s	ˈi	rʲ	ɪ	n	i
s	ˈi	rʲ		n	ɪ
0	0	0	1	0	1

The incorrect alignments of the Levenshtein algorithm with the PMI-generated segment distances are mainly caused by its inability to align vowels with consonants and therefore, just as the VC-sensitive Levenshtein algorithm, it fails to detect metathesis. On the other hand, using segment distances often solves the problem of selecting which of two plausible neighbors a consonant should be aligned with.

Because the PHMM employs segment substitution probabilities, it also often solves the problem of aligning a consonant to one of two neighbors. In addition, the PHMM often correctly aligns metathesis involving equal as well as similar symbols, even realizing an improvement over the Levenshtein swap algorithm. Unfortunately, many wrong alignments of the PHMM are also caused by allowing vowel-consonant alignments. Since the PHMM does not take context into account, it also aligns vowels and consonants which often play a role in metathesis when no metathesis is involved.

6 Discussion

This study provides an alternative evaluation of string distance algorithms by focusing on their effectiveness in aligning segments. We proposed, implemented, and tested the new procedure on a substantial body of data. This provides a new perspective on the quality of distance and alignment algorithms as they have been used in dialectology, where aggregate comparisons had been at times frustratingly inconclusive.

In addition, we introduced the PMI weighting within the Levenshtein algorithm as a simple means of obtaining segment distances, and showed that it improves on the popular Levenshtein algorithm with respect to alignment accuracy.

While the results indicated that the PHMM misaligned the fewest segments, training the PHMM is a lengthy process lasting several hours. Considering that the Levenshtein algorithm with the swap operation and the Levenshtein algorithm with the PMI-generated segment distances are much quicker to (train and) apply, and that they have only slightly lower performance with respect to the segment alignments, we actually prefer using those methods. Another argument in favor of using one of these Levenshtein algorithms is that it is *a priori* clearer what type of alignment errors to expect from them, while the PHMM algorithm is less predictable and harder to comprehend.

While our results are an indication of the good quality of the evaluated algorithms, we only evaluated the algorithms on a single dataset for which a gold standard was available. Ideally we would like to verify these results on other datasets, for which gold standards consisting of multiple or pairwise alignments are available.

Acknowledgements

We are grateful to Peter Kleiweg for extending the Levenshtein algorithm in the L04 package with the swap-operation. We also thank Greg Kondrak for providing the original source code of the Pair Hidden Markov Models. Finally, we thank Therese Leinonen and Sebastian Kürschner of the University of Groningen and Esteve Valls i Alecha of the University of Barcelona for their useful feedback on our ideas.

References

Leonard E. Baum, Ted Petrie, George Soules, and Norman Weiss. 1970. A maximization technique occurring in the statistical analysis of probabilistic functions of Markov Chains. *The Annals of Mathematical Statistics*, 41(1):164–171.

Kenneth W. Church and Patrick Hanks. 1990. Word association norms, mutual information, and lexicography. *Computational Linguistics*, 16(1):22–29.

Fred J. Damerau. 1964. A technique for computer detection and correction of spelling errors. *Communications of the ACM*, 7:171–176.

Richard Durbin, Sean R. Eddy, Anders Krogh, and Graeme Mitchison. 1998. *Biological Sequence Analysis: Probabilistic Models of Proteins and Nucleic Acids*. Cambridge University Press, United Kingdom, July.

Richard Hamming. 1950. Error detecting and error correcting codes. *Bell System Technical Journal*, 29:147–160.

Wilbert Heeringa, Peter Kleiweg, Charlotte Gooskens, and John Nerbonne. 2006. Evaluation of string distance algorithms for dialectology. In John Nerbonne and Erhard Hinrichs, editors, *Linguistic Distances*, pages 51–62, Shroudsburg, PA. ACL.

Wilbert Heeringa. 2004. *Measuring Dialect Pronunciation Differences using Levenshtein Distance*. Ph.D. thesis, Rijksuniversiteit Groningen.

Brett Kessler. 1995. Computational dialectology in Irish Gaelic. In *Proceedings of the seventh conference on European chapter of the Association for Computational Linguistics*, pages 60–66, San Francisco, CA, USA. Morgan Kaufmann Publishers Inc.

Grzegorz Kondrak and Bonnie Dorr. 2003. Identification of Confusable Drug Names: A New Approach and Evaluation Methodology. *Artificial Intelligence in Medicine*, 36:273–291.

Grzegorz Kondrak. 2003. Phonetic Alignment and Similarity. *Computers and the Humanities*, 37:273–291.

Vladimir Levenshtein. 1965. Binary codes capable of correcting deletions, insertions and reversals. *Doklady Akademii Nauk SSSR*, 163:845–848.

Wesley Mackay and Grzegorz Kondrak. 2005. Computing word similarity and identifying cognates with Pair Hidden Markov Models. In *Proceedings of the 9th Conference on Computational Natural Language Learning (CoNLL)*, pages 40–47, Morristown, NJ, USA. Association for Computational Linguistics.

John Nerbonne and Peter Kleiweg. 2007. Toward a dialectological yardstick. *Journal of Quantitative Linguistics*, 14:148–167.

Bruno Pouliquen. 2008. Similarity of names across scripts: Edit distance using learned costs of N-Grams. In Bent Nordström and Aarne Ranta, editors, *Proceedings of the 6th international Conference on Natural Language Processing (GoTal'2008)*, volume 5221, pages 405–416.

Jelena Prokić, Martijn Wieling, and John Nerbonne. 2009. Multiple sequence alignments in linguistics. In Piroska Lendvai and Lars Borin, editors, *Proceedings of the EACL 2009 Workshop on Language Technology and Resources for Cultural Heritage, Social Sciences, Humanities, and Education*.

Lawrence R. Rabiner. 1989. A tutorial on Hidden Markov Models and selected applications in speech recognition. *Proceedings of the IEEE*, 77(2):257–286.

Eric Sven Ristad and Peter N. Yianilos. 1998. Learning string-edit distance. *IEEE Transactions on Pattern Analysis and Machine Intelligence*, 20:522–532.

Robert Wagner and Roy Lowrance. 1975. An extension of the string-to-string correction problem. *Journal of the ACM*, 22(2):177–183.

Martijn Wieling and John Nerbonne. 2007. Dialect pronunciation comparison and spoken word recognition. In Petya Osenova, editor, *Proceedings of the RANLP Workshop on Computational Phonology*, pages 71–78.

Martijn Wieling, Therese Leinonen, and John Nerbonne. 2007. Inducing sound segment differences using Pair Hidden Markov Models. In Mark Ellison John Nerbonne and Greg Kondrak, editors, *Computing and Historical Phonology: 9th Meeting of the ACL Special Interest Group for Computational Morphology and Phonology*, pages 48–56.

A web-enabled and speech-enhanced parallel corpus of Greek - Bulgarian cultural texts

Voula Giouli
Institute for Language & Speech Processing Athens, Greece
voula@ilsp.gr

Nikos Glaros
Institute for Language & Speech Processing Athens, Greece
nglaros@ilsp.gr

Kiril Simov
Institute for Parallel Processing, BAS, Sofia, Bulgaria
kivs@bultreebank.or

Petya Osenova
Institute for Parallel Processing, BAS, Sofia, Bulgaria
petya@bultreebank.org

Abstract

This paper reports on completed work carried out in the framework of an EU-funded project aimed at (a) developing a bilingual collection of cultural texts in Greek and Bulgarian, (b) creating a number of accompanying resources that will facilitate study of the primary texts across languages, and (c) integrating a system which aims to provide web-enabled and speech-enhanced access to digitized bilingual Cultural Heritage resources. This simple user interface, which incorporates advanced search mechanisms, also offers innovative accessibility for visually impaired Greek and Bulgarian users. The rationale behind the work (and the relative resource) was to promote the comparative study of the cultural heritage of the two countries.

1 Introduction

The document describes a bilingual Greek (EL) and Bulgarian (BG) collection of literary and folklore texts along with the metadata that were deemed necessary for the efficient management and retrieval of the textual data. Section 2 outlines the project aims that guided selection and annotation of the texts, whereas Section 3 presents the primary data that comprise the bilingual textual collection and the methodology adopted for collecting them. Section 4 elaborates on the metadata scheme that has been implemented to describe the primary data and the linguistic annotation tailored to facilitate search and retrieval at the document, phrase or word level. This scheme is compliant to widely accepted standards so as to ensure reusability of the resource at hand. Section 5 presents the Language Technologies (LT) deployed in the project elaborating on the Greek and the Bulgarian text processing tools, and discusses the LT methods that have been (a) exploited in the course of the project to facilitate the web-interface construction and (b) integrated in the search and retrieval mechanisms to improve the system performance. Finally, Section 6 describes the main components of the web interface and the way various features are exploited to facilitate users' access to the data. In the last section, we present conclusions and future work.

2 Project description

The project aims at highlighting cultural resources that, as of yet, remain non-exploited to their greatest extent, and at creating the necessary infrastructure with the support of LT with a view to promoting the study of cultural heritage of the eligible neighboring areas and raising awareness about their common cultural identity. To serve these objectives, the project had a concrete target, that is, the creation of a textual collection and of accompanying material that would be appropriate for the promotion and study of the cultural heritage of the neighboring areas in Greece and Bulgaria (Thrace and the neighboring Smolyan, Blagoevgrad, Kardjali, Khaskovo areas), the focus being on literature, folklore and language. To this end, the main activities within the project life-cycle were to:

- record and roadmap the literary production of the afore mentioned areas spanning from the 19th century till the present days along with written records on folk culture and folktales from the eligible areas. These should form a pool of candidate texts from which

Proceedings of the EACL 2009 Workshop on Language Technology and Resources for Cultural Heritage, Social Sciences, Humanities, and Education –LaTeCH – SHELT&R 2009, pages 35–42,
Athens, Greece, 30 March 2009. ©2009 Association for Computational Linguistics

the most appropriate for the project objectives could be selected;

- record and roadmap existing translations of literary works in both languages to serve for the creation of the parallel corpus;
- select textual material representative of the two cultures, and thus, suitable for their comparative study;
- digitize the selected (printed) material to a format suitable for long-term preservation;
- collect meta-texts relevant to the selected literary and folklore texts, that is, texts about the literary works, biographies of the selected authors, criticism, etc.; these comprise part of the accompanying material
- document the data with any information deemed necessary for its preservation and exploitation, catering for their interrelation so as to highlight their common features and allow unified access to the whole set along text types / genres and languages;
- extract bilingual glossaries from the primary collection of literary and folklore texts also accounted for as accompanying material; the project caters for the extraction of EL and BG terms and names of Persons and Locations and their translation equivalents in the other language;
- make the primary resource along with the accompanying material (meta-texts and glossaries) publicly available over the internet to all interested parties, ranging from the research community to laypersons, school students and people interested in finding out more about the particular areas;
- facilitate access to the material that wouldn't be hampered by users' computer literacy and/or language barriers. To cater for the latter, the web interface would be as simple as possible – yet functional – and the data should be available in both languages (Greek and Bulgarian) plus in English.

3 The bilingual Greek – Bulgarian Cultural Corpus

Along with the aforementioned lines, the collection comprises parallel EL – BG literary and folklore texts. The main specifications for the Greek - Bulgarian Cultural Corpus (GBCC) creation were:

- to build a bilingual resource that could be used as a means to study cultural similarities and/or differences between the neighboring areas of Greece and Bulgaria the focus being on literature, folklore and folktales;
- to provide a representative sample of (a) literature written by authors from Thrace -that is from the entire area of Thrace- or about Thrace, spanning between the 19th century - today, (b) folklore texts about Thrace, that would normally reflect cultural as well as linguistic elements either shared by the two people or unique to each culture, and (c) folktales and legends from Thrace, the latter being the intermediate between literature and folklore.

In order to gather the candidate texts and authors for such a collection we exploited both printed and digitized sources, i.e., (on-line and printed) anthologies of Bulgarian, Greek or Balkan literature, digital archives, web resources and library material. The outcome of this extensive research was a wealth of literary works including titles by the most prominent authors in Bulgaria and Greece. The selection of the authors, who would finally participate in GBCC, was based on the following criteria: (a) author's impact to Greek or Bulgarian literature respectively; and (b) author's contribution to his county's folk study or other major sectors such as journalism and education.

Additionally, to ensure corpus “representativeness” to some extend, we tried to include the full range of the literary texts (poetry, fiction, short stories) and in proportion to the literary production with respect to the parameters of place, time and author. To this end, we think we have avoided biases and the corpus models all language varieties spoken in the areas and at different periods.

Moreover, the "inner" content characteristics of texts were used as the basic criteria for text selection. To this end, we chose texts which demonstrate the two people's cultural similarities and affinity along with each author's most important and representative works. Beyond the above, the availability of a translation in the other language and IPR issues also influenced text selection.

The collection of the primary data currently comprises of (135) literary works, (70) BG (Bulgarian) and 65 EL (Greek). Moreover, (30) BG folk texts and 30 EL folk texts along with (25) BG folktales and 31 EL folktales were added in order to build a corpus as balanced as possible and representative of each country's culture. In terms of tokens, the corpus amounts to 700,000 in total (circa 350,000 tokens per language): the literature part is about 550,000 tokens, whereas, the folklore and legend sub-corpus is about 150,000 tokens.

Moreover, to cater for the project requirement that the corpus should be bilingual, available translations of the primary EL – BG literary works were also selected to form the parallel literary corpus. Additionally, an extensive translation work was also carried out by specialized translators where applicable (folklore texts and folktales).

The collection covers EL and BG literary production dating from the 19th century till the present day, and also texts (both literary or folklore) that are written in the dialect(s) used in the eligible areas. This, in effect, is reflected in the language varieties represented in the textual collection that range from contemporary to non-contemporary, and from normal to dialectical or even mixed language.

Finally, the collection of primary data was also coupled with accompanying material (content metadata) for each literary work (literary criticism) and for each author (biographical information, list of works, etc.). Along with all the above, texts about the common cultural elements were also included.

4 Corpus Annotation

After text selection, digitization and extended manual validation (where appropriate) were performed. Normalization of the primary data was kept to a minimum so as to cater, for example, for the conversion from the Greek polytonic to the monotonic encoding system. Furthermore, to ensure efficient content handling and retrieval and also to facilitate access to the resource at hand via the platform that has been developed, metadata descriptions and linguistic annotations were added across two pillars: (a) indexing and retrieval, and (b) further facilitating the comparative study of textual data. To this end, metadata descriptions and linguistic annotations compliant with internationally accepted standards were added to the raw material. The metadata scheme deployed in this project is compliant with internationally accredited standards with certain modifications that cater for the peculiarities of the data.

More specifically, the metadata scheme implemented in this project builds on XCES, the XML version of the Corpus Encoding Standard (XCES, http://www.cs.vassar.edu/XCES/ and CES, http://www.cs.vassar.edu/CES/CES1-0.html), which has been proposed by EAGLES (http://www.ilc.cnr.it/EAGLES96/home.html) and is compliant with the specifications of the Text Encoding Initiative (http://www.tei-c.org, Text Encoding Initiative (TEI Guidelines for Electronic Text Encoding and Interchange). From the total number of elements proposed by these guidelines, the annotation of the parallel corpus at hand has been restricted to the recognition of structural units at the sentence level, which is the minimum level required for the alignment and term extraction processes. That means that the requirements of CES Level 1 conformance are met; as regards CES Level 2 the requirements (but not the recommendations) are also met, and from CES Level 3 requirements, annotation for sentence boundaries is met.

Additionally, metadata elements have been deployed which encode information necessary for text indexing with respect to text title, author, publisher, publication date, etc. (bibliographical information) and for the classification of each text according to text type/genre and topic, the latter being applicable to folklore texts and folk tales. Classification of folklore texts is based on the widely accepted Aarne-Thompson classification system (Aarne, 1961).

To this end, to assure documentation completeness, and facilitate the inter-relation among primary data and the accompanying material (biographies, criticism, etc) the documentation scheme has been extended accordingly. The aforementioned metadata descriptions are kept separately from the data in an xml header that is to be deployed by the web interface for search and retrieval purposes.

The external structural annotation (including text classification) of the corpus also adheres to the IMDI metadata scheme (IMDI, Metadata Elements for Session Descriptions, Version 3.0.4, Sept. 2003). Adaptations proposed specifically concerning Written Language Resources have been taken into account. IMDI metadata elements for catalogue descriptions (IMDI, Metadata Elements for Catalogue Descriptions, Version 2.1, June 2001) were also taken into account to render the corpus compatible with existing formalisms (ELRA, and LDC). This type of metadata descriptions was added manually to the texts.

To further enhance the capabilities/functionalities of the final application, rendering, thus the collection a useful resource to prospective users and researchers, further annotations at various levels of linguistic analysis were integrated across two pillars: (a) efficient indexing and retrieval; and (b) further facilitating the comparative study of textual data by means of bilingual glossaries which were constructed semi-automatically, and via the visualization of aligned parallel texts.

Text processing at the monolingual level comprises the following procedures: (a) handling and tokenization, (b) Part-of-Speech (POS) tagging and lemmatization, (c) surface syntactic analysis, (d) indexing with terms/keywords and phrases/Named Entities (NEs) pertaining to the types Location (LOC) and Person (PER).

Annotations at these levels were added semi-automatically, by deploying existing generic Natural Language Processing (NLP) tools that were developed for the languages at hand, whereas extensive and intensive validations were performed via several ways. Indeed, although the tools deployed have reported to achieve high accuracy rates in the domains/genres they were intended for, the specific nature of the data led to a significant reduction. To this end, half of the annotations were checked manually. After the identification of the errors in this part of the corpus, we have performed a manual check in the second part of the corpus only for these cases which were recognized as errors during the validation of the first part. For some of the cases relevant constraints in the systems were written, which automatically find places where some rules were not met. Tools customization was also performed by adding new rules applicable for the language varieties to be handled, and also by extending/modifying the resources used (word and name lists, etc.).

Finally, alignment of parallel texts (primary source documents and their translations) has also been performed at both sentence and phrase level. As expected, poems posited the major difficulties due the fuzziness in identifying sentence boundaries, and alignments at the phrase level were favored instead.

5 Language Technologies

In what follows the Greek and Bulgarian Text Processing Components will be described.

5.1 The Greek pipe-line

In the case of the Greek data, text processing was applied via an existing pipeline of shallow processing tools for the Greek language. These include:

- Handling and tokenization; following common practice, the Greek tokenizer makes use of a set of regular expressions, coupled with precompiled lists of abbreviations, and a set of simple heuristics (Papageorgiou et al., 2002) for the recognition of word and sentence boundaries, abbreviations, digits, and simple dates.
- POS-tagging and lemmatization; a tagger that is based on Brill's TBL architecture (Brill, 1997), modified to address peculiarities of the Greek language (Papageorgiou et al., 2000) was used in order to assign morphosyntactic information to tokenized words. Furthermore, the tagger uses a PAROLE-compliant tagset of 584 different part-of-speech tags. Following POS tagging, lemmas are retrieved from a Greek morphological lexicon.
- Surface syntactic analysis; the Greek chunker is based on a grammar of 186 rules (Boutsis et al., 2000) developed for the automatic recognition of non-recursive phrasal categories: adjectives, adverbs, prepositional phrases, nouns, verbs (chunks) (Papageorgiou et al., 2002).
- Term extraction; a Greek Term Extractor was used for spotting terms and idiomatic words (Georgantopoulos, Piperidis, 2000). Term Extractor's method proceeds in three pipelined stages: (a) morphosyntactic annotation of the domain corpus, (b) corpus parsing based on a pattern grammar endowed with regular expressions and feature-structure unification, and (c) lemmatization. Candidate terms are then statistically evaluated with an aim to skim valid domain terms and lessen the overgeneration effect caused by pattern grammars (hybrid methodology).

Named Entity Recognition was then performed using MENER (Maximum Entropy Named Entity Recognizer), a system compatible with the ACE (Automatic Content Extraction) scheme, catering for the recognition and classification of the following types of NEs: person (PER), organization (ORG), location (LOC) and geopolitical entity (GPE) (Giouli et al., 2006).

5.2 Bulgarian Tools

In the processing of the Bulgarian part of the corpus we have been using generic language technology tools developed for Bulgarian. Here is the list of tools that we have used. They are implemented within the CLaRK System (Simov et al. 2001) via:

Tokenization, Morphosyntactic tagging, Lemmatization; Tokenization is implemented as a hierarchy of tokenizers within the CLaRK system. Morphosyntactic tagging is done on the basis a morphological lexicon which covers the grammatical information of about 100 000 lexemes (1 600 000 word forms); a gazetteers of about 25000 names and 1500 abbreviations. We are using the BulTreeBank tagset, which is a more specialized version of Multext-east tagset. The disambiguation is done in two steps. Initially, a rule-based module solves the sure cases for which manual rules can be written. Then, for the next step, a neural-network-based disambiguator is being exploited (Simov and Osenova 2001). Lemmatization is implemented as rules which convert each word form in the lemma. The rules are assigned to the word forms in the lexicon. This ensures very high level of accuracy.

Partial Grammars have also been constructed for *Sentence splitting, Named-entity recognition,* and *Chunking*.

5.3 Alignments

To facilitate the comparative study of parallel documents, source texts were automatically aligned with their translations. Alignments at the sentence level were performed semi-automatically by means of the ILSP Aligner, which is a language independent tool that uses surface linguistic information coupled with information about possible unit delimiters depending on the level at which the alignment is sought. The resulting translation equivalents were stored in files conformant to the internationally accredited TMX standard (Translation Memory eXchange, http://www.lisa.org/tmx/), which is XML-compliant, vendor-neutral open standard for storing and exchanging translation memories created by Computer Aided Translation (CAT) and localization tools.

Moreover, terms pertaining to the folklore domain as well as names of Persons and Locations identified in the EL - BG parallel texts were semi-automatically aligned. The outcome of the process of text alignment at below the sentence level was then validated manually.

5.4 Tools Customization and metadata harmonization

As it has already been stated, the tools that were deployed for the linguistic processing are generic ones that were initially developed for different text types/genres. Moreover, the data at hand posed another difficulty that is, coping with older/obsolete language usage. In fact, some of the literary works were written in the 19th century or the beginning of 20th century, and their language reflects the writing standards of the corresponding period.

Therefore, as it was expected, the overall performance of the afore-mentioned tools was lower than the one reported for the texts these tools were initially trained for.

To this end, performance at POS-tagging level dropped from 97% to 77% for the Greek data since no normalization of the primary data was performed. On the other hand, the BG morphological analyzer coverage, whose benchmark performance is 96% dropped to 92 % on poems and folktales and to 94% on literary texts and legends. The reason was that the language of processed literary texts and legends came normalized from the sources, while the poems and folktales kept some percentage of archaic or dialect words. Thus, additionally to the guesser, a post POS processing was performed on the unknown words. Moreover, the accuracy of the neural network disambiguator and the rule-based one was 97 %. i.e. the same as for other applications. Processing at the levels of chunks and NEs were even lower. Within the project we had to tune the tools to the specific language types, such as dia chronically remote texts and domain specific texts (folklore). Also, some words with higher distribution in the target regions appear in some of the works. In order to deal with them we had to extend the used lexicons, to create a guesser for the unknown words and add new rules to the chunk grammar to handle some specific word order within the texts.

Additionally, the deployment of tools that are specific to each language and compatible with completely distinct annotation standards brought about the issue of metadata harmonization. To this end, although the Greek tools were developed to confront to the afore-mentioned annotation standards, this was not the case for Bulgarian. The first encoding scheme followed the BulTreeBank morphological and chunk annotation scheme. Afterwards, the information was transferred into the project scheme in order to be consistent with the Greek data and applicable for web representation. As a result, the morphosyntactic features of the BG tagset, which is a more specialized version of the

Multext-East tagset were mapped onto the relative PAROLE tags.

6 The web interface

All the data collected (being the primary literary or folklore texts or meta-documents, etc.) along with their translations, the multi-layered annotations, and the resulting glossaries were integrated in a database platform that was developed to serve as a content management system. Being the backbone of that platform, the metadata material facilitates the interlinking of similar documents, and the access to the primary data via the web. To this end, a specially designed web site was developed to satisfy the needs of end-users (the general public and the special groups of researchers and other scientists). The website features a trilingual interface (Greek, Bulgarian, English) as well as advanced search and retrieval mechanisms on the entire bilingual content or a user-specified part of it. The users can perform combined searches by author name, title, genre, etc. Furthermore, they can search for single keywords/wordforms or for two wordforms that can be a user-specified number of words apart from each other. Searches by lemma and/or by phrase have been also implemented. The latter rely on a matcher, which tries to link the query word(s) with the stored lemmas/wordforms. Additionally, a stemmer for Greek and Bulgarian has been used for the online stemming of queries, which will then be matched with the already stemmed corpus. When all the above fails, fuzzy matching techniques are being employed, facilitating, thus, effective query expansion functionality. Finally, apart from wordforms and lemmas, the collection can also be queried for morphosyntactic tags or any combination thereof; results, then, come in the form of concordances and statistics (frequency information), hence the relative document(s) can also be retrieved. Moreover, users can search the whole corpus or define a sub-corpus based on the classification and annotation parameters accompanying each text, thus, creating sub-corpora of a specific author, or belonging to a specific genre, text type, domain, time period, etc.

In addition, the web interface lets the users to simultaneously view on screen both Greek and Bulgarian texts, aligned and in parallel,, so that to become acquainted with the comparative aspects of the two languages or perform specific linguistic, lexicographic or translation tasks. Alternatively, the user can consult the bilingual glossary of terms and the aligned list of NEs. The latter is often very interesting, especially with respect to Location entities, since transliteration is usually non-adequate.

The design of the web interface effectively blends simplicity and advanced functionality so that to fully support the intended usage scenarios (comparative study of literary and folklore texts equally by specialists, laymen or students, language and/or literary teaching and learning, lexicographic projects, etc.). Finally, the web interface has been enhanced by integrating last generation of synthetic speech technology for both Greek and Bulgarian. This speech-enhanced user interface (S. Raptis et al, 2005), offers innovative web accessibility for blind and vision impaired Greek and Bulgarian users as well as for other users who use speech as their preferable modality to information access. The key-feature of this web-speech technology is that it lets users to interact with the underlying system; so that they can hear only the portions of a specific web page they are interested in, being able at the same time to navigate through the entire web site and visit only the web pages of their choice.

7 Conclusions and future work

We have described work targeted at the promotion and study of the cultural heritage of the cross-border regions of Greece – Bulgaria, the focus been on literature, folklore and language of the two people, by means of modern and technologically advanced platforms. To this end, a digital collection of literary and folklore texts has been compiled along with accompanying material selected from various (online and printed sources), which is integrated into a platform with advanced search and retrieval mechanisms.

However, the cultural value of the bilingual cultural Greek-Bulgarian corpus goes beyond the border areas that it was intended for, because it shows the similarities and the differences between the two neighboring countries. More specifically, it can be used for supporting the acquisition of the other language in both countries. Also, it can be explored for comparing the cultural and social attitudes in diachronic depth and genre variety. Apart from the usages from a humanities point of view, the corpus can become a good base for testing taggers, parsers and aligners. It would especially challenge the processing of the regional dialects, the language of poems, and the language of non-contemporary works.

Future work is being envisaged in the following directions: extending the corpus with more texts, and respectively the glossaries – with more terms, adding more layers of linguistic analysis (predicate-argument structure, etc.), and further enhance search and retrieval with the construction and deployment of an applicable thesaurus.

Acknowledgments

We would like to thank the anonymous reviewers for useful suggestions and comments. Most of the work presented in this paper was done in the framework of a project that was funded under the Community Initiative Programme INTERREG III A / PHARE CBC Greece – Bulgaria. The project was implemented by the Institute for Language and Speech Processing (ILSP, www.ilsp.gr) and a group of academics and researchers from the Sofia University St. Kliment Ohridski (www.uni-sofia.bg).

References

Antti Aarne. 1961. *The Types of the Folktale: A Classification and Bibliography. Translated and Enlarged by Stith Thompson.* 2nd rev. ed. Helsinki: Suomalainen Tiedeakatemia / FF Communications.

Sotiris Boutsis, Prokopis Prokopidis, Voula Giouli and Stelios Piperidis. 2000. *A Robust Parser for Unrestricted Greek Tex.* In Proceedings of the 2nd Language and Resources Evaluation Conference, 467-473, Athens, Greece.

Michel Généreux. 2007. Cultural Heritage Digital Resources: From Extraction to Querying, Language Technology for Cultural Heritage Data (LaTeCH 2007), Workshop at ACL 2007, June 23rd–30th 2007, Prague, Czech Republic.

Byron Georgantopoulos and Stelios Piperidis, 2000. *Term-based Identification of Sentences for Text Summarization.* In Proceedings of LREC2000

Voula Giouli, Alexis Konstandinidis, Elina Desypri, Harris Papageorgiou. 2006. *Multi-domain Multilingual Named Entity Recognition: Revisiting & Grounding the resources issue.* In Proceedings of LREC 2006.

IMDI, Metadata Elements for Catalogue Descriptions, Version 2.1, June 2001

IMDI, Metadata Elements for Session Descriptions, Version 3.0.4, Sept. 2003.

Harris Papageorgiou, L. Cranias, Stelios Piperidis1994. *Automatic alignment in parallel corpora.* In Proceedings of ACL 1994.

Harris Papageorgiou, Prokopis Prokopidis, Voula Giouli, Iasonas Demiros, Alexis Konstantinidis, and Stelios Piperidis. 2002. *Multi-level XML-based Corpus Annotation.* Proceedings of the 3nd Language and Resources Evaluation Conference.

Harris Papageorgiou, Prokopis Prokopidis, Voula Giouli, and Stelios Piperidis. 2000. *A Unified POS Tagging Architecture and its Application to Greek.* In Proceedings of the 2nd Language and Resources Evaluation Conference, Athens, Greece, pp 1455-1462.

Stelios Piperidis. 1995. *Interactive corpus based translation drafting tool.* In ASLIB Proceedings 47(3), March 1995.

Spyros Raptis, I. Spais and P. Tsiakoulis. 2005. *A Tool for Enhancing Web Accessibility: Synthetic Speech and Content Restructuring".* In Proc. HCII 2005: 11th International Conference on Human-Computer Interaction, 22-27 July, Las Vegas, Nevada, USA.

Kiril Simov, Z. Peev, M. Kouylekov, A. Simov, M. Dimitrov, and A. Kiryakov. 2001. *CLaRK - an XML-based System for Corpora Development.* Corpus Linguistics 2001 Conference. pp 558-560.

Kiril Simov, and Petya Osenova. *A Hybrid System for MorphoSyntactic Disambiguation in Bulgarian.* In: Proc. of the RANLP 2001 Conference, Tzigov Chark, Bulgaria, 5-7 September 2001. pages 288-290.

René Witte, Thomas Gitzinger, Thomas Kappler, and Ralf Krestel. 2008. A Semantic Wiki Approach to Cultural Heritage Data Management. Language Technology for Cultural Heritage Data (LaTeCH 2008), Workshop at LREC 2008, June 1st, 2008, Marrakech, Morocco.

The Development of the *Index Thomisticus* Treebank Valency Lexicon

Barbara McGillivray
University of Pisa
Italy
b.mcgillivray@ling.unipi.it

Marco Passarotti
Catholic University of the Sacred Heart
Milan, Italy
marco.passarotti@unicatt.it

Abstract

We present a valency lexicon for Latin verbs extracted from the *Index Thomisticus* Treebank, a syntactically annotated corpus of Medieval Latin texts by Thomas Aquinas.
In our corpus-based approach, the lexicon reflects the empirical evidence of the source data. Verbal arguments are induced directly from annotated data.
The lexicon contains 432 Latin verbs with 270 valency frames. The lexicon is useful for NLP applications and is able to support annotation.

1 Introduction

Over the last decades, annotated corpora and computational lexicons have gained an increasing role among language resources in computational linguistics: on the one hand, they are used to train Natural Language Processing (NLP) tools such as parsers and PoS taggers; on the other hand, they are developed through automatic procedures of linguistic annotation and lexical acquisition.

The relation between annotated corpora and computational lexicons is circular: as a matter of fact, if linguistic annotation of textual data is supported and improved by the use of lexicons, these latter can be induced from annotated data in a corpus-based fashion.

In the field of cultural heritage and in particular that of classical languages studies, much effort has been devoted throughout the years to the digitization of texts, but only recently have some projects begun to annotate them above the morphological level.

Concerning lexicology and lexicography of classical languages, a long tradition has produced and established many dictionaries, thesauri and lexicons, providing examples from real texts. Nevertheless, nowadays it is possible and indeed necessary to match lexicons with data from (annotated) corpora, and viceversa. This requires the scholars to exploit the vast amount of textual data from classical languages already available in digital format,[1] and particularly those annotated at the highest levels. The evidence provided by the texts themselves can be fully represented in lexicons induced from these data. Subsequently, these lexicons can be used to support the textual annotation itself in a virtuous circle.

This paper reports on the creation of a valency lexicon induced from the *Index Thomisticus* Treebank, a syntactically annotated corpus of Medieval Latin texts by Thomas Aquinas. The paper is organised as follows: section 2 describes the available Latin treebanks, their annotation guidelines and gives some specific information on the Index Thomisticus treebank; section 3 deals with the notion of valency, while section 4 describes the state of the art on valency lexicons; section 5 illustrates the procedures of acquisition and representation of our valency lexicon; finally, section 6 draws some conclusions and describes future work.

2 Latin Treebanks

Latin is a richly inflected language, showing:

- discontinuous constituents ('non-projectivity'): this means that phrasal constituents may not be continuous, but broken up by words of other constituents. An example is the following sentence by Ovid (Metamorphoses, I.1-2): "In nova fert animus mutatas dicere formas corpora" ("My mind leads me to tell of forms changed into new bodies"). In this sentence, both the nominal phrases "nova corpora" and "mutatas formas" are discontinuous;
- moderately free word-order: for instance, the order of the words in a sentence like "au-

[1] See, for instance, the Perseus Digital Library (Crane et al., 2001), or data repositories such as LASLA (Denooz, 1996).

Proceedings of the EACL 2009 Workshop on Language Technology and Resources for Cultural Heritage, Social Sciences, Humanities, and Education –LaTeCH – SHELT&R 2009, pages 43–50,
Athens, Greece, 30 March 2009.

daces fortuna iuvat" ("fortune favours the bold") could be changed into "fortuna audaces iuvat", or "fortuna iuvat audaces", without affecting the meaning of the sentence.

These features of Latin influenced the choice of Dependency Grammars (DG)[2] as the most suitable grammar framework for building Latin annotated corpora like treebanks.

While since the 1970s the first treebanks were annotated via Phrase Structure Grammar (PSG)-based schemata (as in IBM, Lancaster and, later on, Penn treebanks), in the past decade many projects of dependency treebanks development have started, such as the ALPINO treebank for Dutch (Van der Beek et al., 2002), the Turin University Treebank for Italian (Lesmo et al., 2002), or the Danish Dependency Treebank (Kromann, 2003). On the one hand, this is due to the fact that the first treebanks were mainly English language corpora. PSG were a suitable framework for a poorly inflected language like English, showing a fixed word-order and few discontinuous constituents. Later on, the syntactic annotation of moderately free word-order languages required the adoption of the DG framework, which is more appropriate than PSG for such a task. On the other hand, Carroll et al. (1998) showed that inter-annotator agreement was significantly better for dependency treebanks, indicating that phrase structure annotation was requiring too many irrelevant decisions (see also Lin, 1995).

Although much Latin data is nowadays available in digital format, the first two projects for the development of Latin treebanks have only recently started: namely the Latin Dependency Treebank (LDT) at the Tufts University in Boston (within the Perseus Digital Library) based on texts of the Classical era (Bamman, 2006), and the Index Thomisticus Treebank (IT-TB) at the Catholic University of the Sacred Heart in Milan, based on the *Opera omnia* of Thomas Aquinas (Passarotti, 2007).

Taking into account the above mentioned features of Latin, both the treebanks independently chose the DG framework as the most suitable one for data annotation. The same approach was later on followed by a third Latin treebank now available, which is ongoing at the University of Oslo in the context of the PROIEL project (Pragmatic Resources in Old Indo-European Languages): the aim of PROIEL is the syntactic annotation of the oldest extant versions of the New Testament in Indo-European languages, including Greek, Latin, Gothic, Armenian and Church Slavonic (Haug and Jøhndal, 2008).

2.1 Annotation Guidelines

Since LDT and IT-TB were the first projects of their kind for Latin, no prior established guidelines were available to rely on for syntactic annotation.

Therefore, the so-called 'analytical layer' of annotation of the Prague Dependency Treebank (PDT) for Czech (Hajič et al., 1999) was chosen and adapted to specific or idiosyncratic constructions of Latin. These constructions (such as the ablative absolute or the passive periphrastic) could be syntactically annotated in several different ways and are common to Latin of all eras. Rather than have each treebank project decide upon and record each decision for annotating them, LDT and IT-TB decided to pool their resources and create a single annotation manual that would govern both treebanks (Bamman et al., 2007a; Bamman et al., 2007b; Bamman et al., 2008).

As we are dealing with Latin dialects separated by 13 centuries, sharing a single annotation manual is very useful for comparison purposes, such as checking annotation consistency or diachronically studying specific syntactic constructions. In addition, the task of data annotation through these common guidelines allows annotators to base their decisions on a variety of examples from a wider range of texts and combine the two datasets in order to train probabilistic dependency parsers.

Although the PROIEL annotation guidelines are grounded on the same grammar framework as the LDT and IT-TB, they differ in a number of details, some of which are described in Passarotti (forthcoming).

2.2 The *Index Thomisticus* Treebank

The *Index Thomisticus* (IT) by Roberto Busa SJ (1974-1980) was begun in 1949 and is considered a groundbreaking project in computational linguistics. It is a database containing the *Opera omnia* of Thomas Aquinas (118 texts) as well as 61 texts by other authors related to Thomas, for a total of around 11 million tokens. The corpus is morphologically tagged and lemmatised.

[2] With Tesnière (1959) as a common background, there are many different current DG flavours. See for instance the following: Dependency Unification Grammar (Hellwig, 1986), Functional Generative Description (Sgall, Hajičová and Panevová, 1986), Meaning Text Theory (Mel'čuk, 1988), Word Grammar (Hudson, 1990).

Early in the 1970's Busa started to plan a project aimed at both the morphosyntactic disambiguation of the IT lemmatisation and the syntactic annotation of its sentences. Today, these tasks are performed by the IT-TB project, which is part of the wider 'Lessico Tomistico Biculturale', a project whose target is the development of a lexicon from the IT texts.[3]

Presently, the size of the IT-TB is 46,456 tokens, for a total of 2,103 parsed sentences excerpted from the *Scriptum super Sententiis Magistri Petri Lombardi*.

3 Valency

As outlined above, the notion of valency is generally defined as the number of complements required by a word: these obligatory complements are usually named 'arguments', while the non-obligatory ones are referred to as 'adjuncts'. Although valency can refer to different parts of speech (usually verbs, nouns and adjectives), scholars have mainly focused their attention on verbs, so that the notion of valency often coincides with verbal valency.

Valency is widely used in DG formalisms, but it also figures in PSG-based formalisms like HPSG and LFG.

While Karl Bühler can be considered as the pioneer of the modern theory of valency,[4] Lucien Tesnière is widely recognised as its real founder. Tesnière views valency as a quantitative quality of verbs, since only verbs constrain both the quantity and the quality (i.e. nouns and adverbs) of their obligatory arguments; through a metaphor borrowed from drama, Tesnière classifies dependents into *actants* (arguments) and *circonstants* (adjuncts): "Le noeud verbal [...] exprime tout un petit drame. Comme un drame en effet, il comporte obligatoirement un procès, et le plus souvent des acteurs et des circonstances. Transposés du plan de la réalité dramatique sur celui de la syntaxe structurale, le procès, les acteurs et les circonstances deviennent respectivement le verbe, les actants et les circonstants" (Tesnière, 1959: 102).[5]

Arguments can be either obligatory or optional, depending on which sense of the verb is involved. For example, the *seem* sense of the verb *appear* requires two obligatory arguments in active clauses, as in the following sentence: "That lawyer appears to love his work". Here the second argument ("to love his work") cannot be left out without changing the meaning of the verb. On the other hand, optional arguments are recorded into the verbal argument structure itself, althought they may not appear at the clausal level. For instance, in the following sentence the object required by the verb *eat* is missing, but the sentence is still acceptable: "He eats (something)".

Optionality can also act at the communicative level as well as at the structural one. For instance, adjuncts can be necessary for communicative intelligibility in particular contexts, as in the following sentence: "I met James at the Marquee club", where the locative adverbial ("at the Marquee club") is required to answer a question like "Where did you meet James?". On the other hand, structural optionality depends on the features of the language and applies at the clausal level. For instance, as a poorly inflected language, English requires the subject of a predicate to be expressed in declarative and interrogative main clauses, so that a sentence like the following is ungrammatical if the subject is missing: "[I] slept all morning".

Given the so-called "syntax-semantics interface" (Levin, 1993), arguments are generally associated with a predicate sense rather than a predicate form, and are structured in sequences called 'subcategorization frames' (SCFs) or 'complementation patterns'. For example, there is a semantic difference between the *bill* sense and the *attack* sense of the verb *charge* in English, as in the following sentences:

- (a) "The hotel charges 80 euros for a night".
- (b) "The army charged the enemy".

In these sentences, the two predicate senses show two different SCFs:

- (a) [Subj_NP, Pred, Obj_NP, Obj_PP-for]
- (b) [Pred, Obj_NP]

Arguments are also selected by verbs according to lexical-semantic properties, called 'selectional preferences' (SPs) or 'selectional restrictions'. For example, a sentence like "*The train flew to Rome" is ungrammatical, since it violates

---

[3] http://itreebank.marginalia.it.

[4] In the *Sprachtheorie*, he writes that "die Wörter einer bestimmten Wortklasse eine oder mehrere Leerstellen um sich eröffnen, die durch Wörter bestimmter anderer Wortklassen ausgefüllt werden müssen" (Bühler, 1934: 173) ("words of a certain word-class open up around themselves one or several empty spaces that have to be filled by words of certain other word-classes"; our translation).

[5] "The verbal node expresses a whole little drama. As a drama, it implies a process and, most of the times, actors and circumstances. Transposed from the dramatic reality to structural syntax, the process, the actors and the circumstances respectively become the verb, the actants and the circumstants" (our translation).

the SP of the verb *fly* on its subject and can only be accepted in a metaphorical context.

4 Valency Lexicons

Over the past years, several valency lexicons have been built within different theoretical frameworks: these lexicons have an important role in the NLP community thanks to their wide applications in NLP components, such as parsing, word sense disambiguation, automatic verb classification and selectional preference acquisition.

As shown in Urešová (2004), a valency lexicon can also help the task of linguistic annotation (as in treebank development), providing annotators with essential information about the number and types of arguments realized at the syntactic level for a specific verb, along with semantic information on the verb's lexical preferences.

In the phase of lexicon creation, both intuition-based and corpus-based approaches can be pursued, according to the role played by human intuition and empirical evidence extracted from annotated corpora such as treebanks.

For instance, lexicons like PropBank (Kingsbury and Palmer, 2002), FrameNet (Ruppenhofer et al., 2006) and PDT-Vallex (Hajič et al., 2003) have been created in an intuition-based fashion and then checked and improved with examples from corpora.

On the other side, research in lexical acquisition has recently made available a number of valency lexicons automatically acquired from annotated corpora, such as VALEX (Korhonen, et al., 2006) and LexShem (Messiant et al., 2008). Unlike the fully intuition-based ones, these lexicons aim at systematically reflecting the evidence provided by data, with very little human intervention. The role of intuition is therefore left to the annotation phase (where the annotator interprets the corpus data), and not extended to the development of the lexicon itself.

Corpus-based lexicons show several advantages if compared with traditional human-developed dictionaries. Firstly, they systematically reflect the evidence of the corpus they were extracted from, while acquiring information specific to the domain of the corpus. Secondly, unlike manually built lexicons, they are not prone to human errors that are difficult to detect, such as omissions and inconsistencies. In addition, such lexicons usually display statistical information in their entries, such as the actual frequency of subcategorization frames as attested in the original corpus. Finally, they are less costly than hand-crafted lexical resources in terms of time, money and human resources.

While several subcategorization lexicons have been compiled for modern languages, much work in this field still remains to be done on classical languages such as Greek and Latin. Regarding Latin, Happ reports a list of Latin verbs along with their valencies (Happ, 1976: 480-565). Bamman and Crane (2008) describe a "dynamic lexicon" automatically extracted from the Perseus Digital Library, using the LDT as a training set. This lexicon displays qualitative and quantitative information on subcategorization patterns and selectional preferences of each word as it is used in every Latin author of the corpus. Relying on morphological tagging and statistical syntactic parsing of such a large corpus, their approach finds the most common arguments and the most common lexical fillers of these arguments, thus reducing the noise caused by the automatic pre-processing of the data.

5 The *Index Thomisticus* Treebank Valency Lexicon

We propose a corpus-based valency lexicon for Latin verbs automatically induced from IT-TB data. The automatic procedure allows both the extension of this work to the LDT (thanks to the common annotation guidelines) and the updating of the lexicon as the treebank size increases.

First, we automatically extract the arguments of all the occurrences of verbal lemmata in the treebank, along with their morphological features and lexical fillers.

In the IT-TB, verbal arguments are annotated using the following tags: Sb (Subject), Obj (Object), OComp (Object Complement) and Pnom (Predicate Nominal); adjuncts are annotated with the tag Adv (Adverbial). The difference between Obj and Adv corresponds to the that between direct or indirect arguments (except subjects) and adjuncts. A special kind of Obj is the determining complement of the object, which is tagged with OComp, such as *senatorem* in the phrase "aliquem senatorem facere" ("to nominate someone senator"). Conversely, the determining complement of the subject is tagged as Pnom, as in "aliquis senator fit" ("someone becomes senator").[6]

[6] As in the PDT, all of the syntactic tags can be appended with a suffix in the event that the given node is member of a coordinated construction (_Co), an apposition (_Ap) or a parenthetical statement (_Pa).

In order to retrieve the arguments realised for each verbal occurrence in the treebank, specific database queries have been created to search for the nodes depending on a verbal head through the functional tags listed above.

The head-dependent relation can be either direct or indirect, since intermediate nodes may intervene. These nodes are prepositions (tag AuxP), conjunctions (tag AuxC) and coordinating or apposing elements (respectively, tags Coord and Apos).

For example, see the following sentences:

- [1] "primo determinat formam baptismi;"[7] ("at first it determines the form of the baptism;")
- [2] "ly aliquid autem, et ly unum non determinant aliquam formam vel naturam;"[8] ("the 'something' and the 'one' do not determine any form or nature")

Figure 1 reports the tree of sentence [1], where the Obj relation between the verbal head *determinat* and the dependent *formam* is direct.

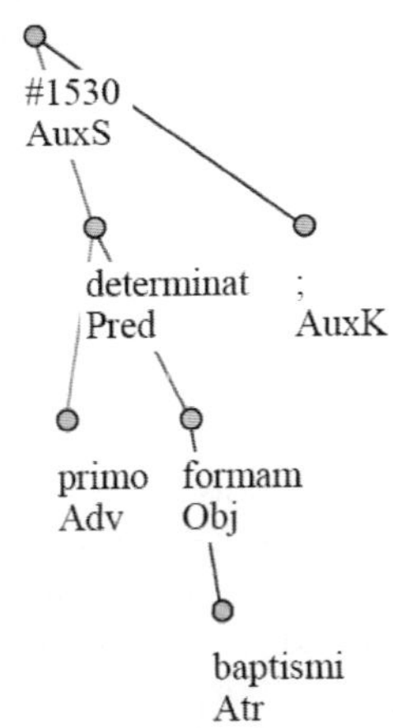

Figure 1.
Tree of sentence [1]

Figure 2 shows the tree of sentence [2]. In this tree, two coordinated subjects (*aliquid* and *unum*) and two coordinated objects (*formam* and *naturam*) depend on the common verbal head *determinant* through two different Coord nodes (*et* and *vel*)[9].

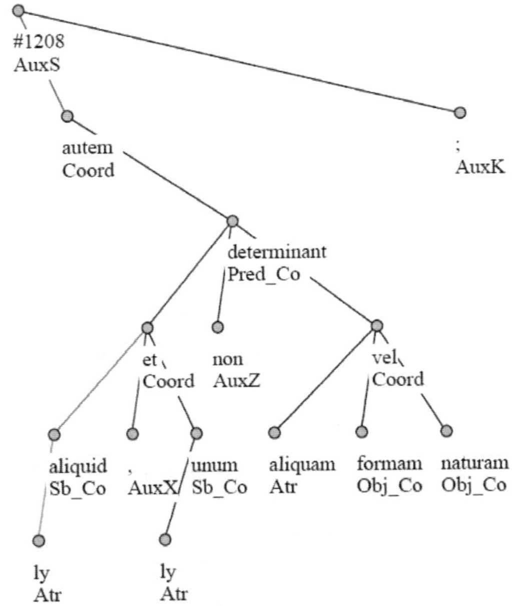

Figure 2
Tree of sentence [2]

In the case of indirect relation, the intermediate nodes need to be detected and extracted, in order to be inserted into the lexicon as subcategorization structures containing the syntactic roles of the verbal arguments. To represent these structures, we distinguished two major types of them: subcategorization frames (SCFs) and subcategorization classes (SCCs).

An SCF contains the sequence of functional labels of verbal arguments as they appear in the sentence order, whereas an SCC reports the subcategorization elements disregarding their linear order in the sentence. SCFs and SCCs play a different role in our lexicon. On the one hand, SCFs are very detailed patterns useful for diachronic and/or comparative studies on linear order. On the other hand, SCCs are more general and make the data in the lexicon comparable with the subcategorization structures as usually defined in the literature and in other valency lexicons. For each of these structures we then created the following sub-types, ranging from the most specific to the least specific one.

SCF_1: subcategorization frame marking the full path between the verbal head (referred to as 'V') and each of its argument nodes in the tree. SCF_1 also assigns the same index to those argument nodes linked by coordinating or apposing elements. For instance, the SCF_1 of the verbal

[7] Thomas, *Super Sententiis Petri Lombardi*, IV, Distinctio 3, Quaestio 1, Prologus, 41-6, 42-2. The edition of the text recorded in the IT is Thomas (1856-1858).

[8] Thomas, *Super Sententiis Petri Lombardi*, III, Distinctio 6, Quaestio 2, Articulus 1, Responsio ad Argumentum 7, 4-5, 6-1.

[9] Following PDT-style, the distributed determination *aliquam*, which modifies both the coordinated objects *formam* and *naturam*, depends on the coordinating node *vel*. For more details, see Hajic et al. (1999), 236-238.

head *determino*[10] in sentence [1] is 'V + Obj', while in sentence [2] is '(Coord)Sb_Co$^{(1)}$ + (Coord)Sb_Co$^{(1)}$ + V + (Coord)Obj_Co$^{(2)}$ + (Coord)Obj_Co$^{(2)}$'. In the latter, the intermediate nodes Coord are in square brackets and indices *1* and *2* link the coordinated nodes. These indices have been adopted in order to disambiguate subcategorization structures where more Obj_Co tags can refer to different verbal arguments. For instance, in a sentence like "I give X and Y to W and Z", both the tranferred objects (X and Y) and the receivers (W and Z) are annotated with Obj_Co. Using indices, the subcategorization structure of the verb *give* in this sentence appears as follows: 'Sb + V + (Coord)Obj_Co$^{(1)}$ + (Coord)Obj_Co$^{(1)}$ + (Coord)Obj_Co$^{(2)}$ + (Coord)Obj_Co$^{(2)}$'. The indices cannot be applied *a priori* to subsequent arguments, since Latin, allowing discontinuous constituents, can show cases where coindexed nodes are separated by other lexical items in the linear order.

SCC_1: the subcategorization class associated with SCF_1. The SCC_1 of the verb *determino* in [1] is '{Obj}', while in [2] is '{(Coord)Sb_Co$^{(1)}$, (Coord)Sb_Co$^{(1)}$, (Coord)Obj_Co$^{(2)}$, (Coord)Obj_Co$^{(2)}$}'.

SCF_2: a subcategorization frame containing only the labels and the indices of the arguments, but not the full path. So, the SCF_2 of *determino* in [1] is 'V + Obj', while in [2] is 'Sb_Co$^{(1)}$ + Sb_Co$^{(1)}$ + V + Obj_Co$^{(2)}$ + Obj_Co$^{(2)}$'.

SCC_2: the subcategorization class associated with SCF_2. For *determino*, this is '{Obj}' in [1] and '{Sb_Co$^{(1)}$, Sb_Co$^{(1)}$, Obj_Co$^{(2)}$, Obj_Co$^{(2)}$}' in [2].

SCC_3: a subcategorization frame containing only the argument labels. The SCC_3 of *determino* is '{Obj}' in [1] and '{Sb, Obj}' in [2], showing that in this sentence *determino* is used as a biargumental verb, regardless of the number of lexical fillers realised for each of its arguments at the surface level.

6 Conclusion and future work

Presently, the size of the IT-TB valency lexicon is 432 entries (i.e. verbal lemmata, corresponding to 5966 wordforms), with 270 different SCF_1s. In the near future, the lexicon will be enriched with valency information for nouns and adjectives.

The corpus-based approach we followed induces verbal arguments directly from annotated data, where the arguments may be present or not, depending on the features of the texts. Therefore, the lexicon reflects the empirical evidence given by the data it was extracted from, encouraging linguistic studies on the particular language domain of our corpus.

In addition to the syntactic information reported in the different types of SCFs and SCCs, it is possible at each stage to include both the morphological features and the lexical fillers of verbal arguments, helping define verbal selectional preferences.

The lexicon may also be useful for improving the performance of statistical parsers, enriching the information acquired by parsers on verbal entries. On the other hand, moving from parser performance to lexicon development, the lexicon can be induced from automatically parsed texts when an accurate parsing system is available.

The syntactic and lexical data recorded in the lexicon are also important in further semantic NLP applications, such as word sense disambiguation, anaphora and ellipsis resolution, and selectional preference acquisition. Following a widespread approach in valency lexicons, a close connection between valency frames and word senses will be followed in the description of lexicon entries: this means that each headword entry of our lexicon will consist of one or more SCFs and SCCs, one for each sense of the word.

We plan to make the lexicon available online through a graphical interface usable also during the annotation procedures, as has been already done for the PDT via the tree editor TrEd.[11] In this way, the consistency of the annotation process can be tested and enforced thanks to the information stored in the lexicon.

In order to test the accuracy of our system, it will be also necessary to evaluate the quality of our valency lexicon against the Perseus "dynamic lexicon", Happ's list and other existing resources for Latin, such as traditional dictionaries and thesauri. A comparison with the lexicon by Perseus is also very interesting in a contrastive diachronic perspective, as it may show important linguistic differences between Classical and Medieval Latin.

Acknowledgments

We would like to thank Paolo Ruffolo for his help in designing the database architecture.

References

[10] *Determino* is the lemma of both the wordforms *determinat* (sentence [1]) and *determinant* (sentence [2]).

[11] TrEd is freely available at http://ufal.mff.cuni.cz/~pajas/tred/.

David Bamman. 2006. The Design and Use of Latin Dependency Treebank. In Jan Hajič and Joakim Nivre (eds.), *TLT 2006. Proceedings of the Fifth Workshop on Treebanks and Linguistic Theories. December 1-2, 2006, Prague, Czech Republic*, Institute of Formal and Applied Linguistics, Prague, Czech Republic, 67-78.

David Bamman and Gregory Crane. 2008. Building a Dynamic Lexicon from a Digital Library. In *Proceedings of the 8th ACM/IEEE-CS Joint Conference on Digital Libraries (JCDL 2008)*, Pittsburgh.

David Bamman, Marco Passarotti, Gregory Crane and Savina Raynaud. 2007a. *Guidelines for the Syntactic Annotation of Latin Treebanks*, «Tufts University Digital Library». Available at: http://dl.tufts.edu/view_pdf.jsp?urn=tufts:facpubs:dbamma01-2007.00002.

David Bamman, Marco Passarotti, Gregory Crane and Savina Raynaud. 2007b. A Collaborative Model of Treebank Development. In Koenraad De Smedt, Jan Hajič and Sandra Kübler (eds.), *Proceedings of the Sixth International Workshop on Treebanks and Linguistic Theories. December 7-8, 2007, Bergen, Norway*, Northern European Association for Language Technology (NEALT) Proceedings Series, Vol. 1, 1-6.

David Bamman, Marco Passarotti, Roberto Busa and Gregory Crane. 2008. The annotation guidelines of the Latin Dependency Treebank and *Index Thomisticus* Treebank. The treatment of some specific syntactic constructions in Latin. In *Proceedings of the Sixth International Conference on Language Resources and Evaluation (LREC 2008). May 28-30, 2008, Marrakech, Morocco*, European Language Resources Association (ELRA), 2008.

Karl Bühler. 1934. *Sprachtheorie: die Darstellungsfunktion der Sprache*, Jena: Gustav Fischer, Stuttgart.

Roberto Busa. 1974–1980. *Index Thomisticus: sancti Thomae Aquinatis operum omnium indices et concordantiae, in quibus verborum omnium et singulorum formae et lemmata cum suis frequentiis et contextibus variis modis referuntur quaeque / consociata plurium opera atque electronico IBM automato usus digessit Robertus Busa SJ*, Frommann-Holzboog, Stuttgart-Bad Cannstatt.

Gregory R. Crane, Robert F. Chavez, Anne Mahoney, Thomas L. Milbank, Jeff A. Rydberg-Cox, David A. Smith and Clifford E. Wulfman. 2001. Drudgery and deep thought: Designing a digital library for the humanities. In *Communications of the ACM*, 44(5), 34-40.

John Carroll, Ted Briscoe and Antonio Sanfilippo. 1998. Parser Evaluation: a Survey and a New Proposal. In *Proceedings of the First International Conference on Language Resources and Evaluation (LREC 1998). May 28-30, 1998, Granada, Spain*, 447-454.

Joseph Denooz. 1996. *La banque de données du laboratoire d'analyse statistique des langues anciennes (LASLA)*. « Le Médiéviste et l'ordinateur », 33, 14-20.

Jan Hajič, Jarmila Panevová, Eva Buráňová, Zdeňka Urešová and Alla Bémová. 1999. *Annotations at Analytical Level. Instructions for annotators*, Institute of Formal and Applied Linguistics, Prague, Czech Republic. Available at: http://ufal.mff.cuni.cz/pdt2.0/doc/manuals/en/a-layer/pdf/a-man-en.pdf.

Jan Hajič, Jarmila Panevová, Zdeňka Urešová, Alla Bémová, Veronika Kolárová-Reznícková and Petr Pajas. 2003. PDT-VALLEX: Creating a Large Coverage Valency Lexicon for Treebank Annotation. In Joakim Nivre and Erhard Hinrichs (eds.), *TLT 2003 – Proceedings of the Second Workshop on Treebanks and Linguistic Theories*, volume 9 of *Mathematical Modelling in Physics, Engineering and Cognitive Sciences*, Växjö University Press, Växjö, Sweden, 57-68.

Heinz Happ. 1976. *Grundfragen einer Dependenz-Grammatik des Lateinischen*, Vandenhoeck & Ruprecht, Goettingen.

Dag Haug and Marius Jøhndal. 2008. Creating a Parallel Treebank of the Old Indo-European Bible Translations. In *Proceedings of the Language Technology for Cultural Heritage Data Workshop (LaTeCH 2008), Marrakech, Morocco, 1st June 2008*, 27-34.

Peter Hellwig. 1986. Dependency Unification Grammar, In *Proceedings of the 11th International Conference on Computational Linguistics*, Universität Bonn, Bonn, 195-198.

Richard Hudson. 1990. *English Word Grammar*, Blackwell Publishers Ltd, Oxford, UK.

Paul Kingsbury and Martha Palmer. 2002. From Treebank to Propbank. In *Proceedings of the Third International Conference on Language Resources and Evaluation (LREC 2002)*, Las Palmas – Gran Canaria, Spain.

Anna Korhonen, Yuval Krymolowski and Ted Briscoe. 2006. A Large Subcategorization Lexicon for Natural Language Processing Applications. In *Proceedings of the Fifth International Conference on Language Resources and Evaluation (LREC 2006)*, Genoa, Italy.

Matthias T. Kromann. 2003. The Danish Dependency Treebank and the underlying linguistic theory. In Joakim Nivre and Erhard Hinrichs (eds.), *TLT 2003 – Proceedings of the Second Workshop on Treebanks and Linguistic Theories*, volume 9 of *Mathematical Modelling in Physics, Engineering and Cognitive Sciences*, Växjö University Press, Växjö, Sweden.

Leonardo Lesmo, Vincenzo Lombardo and Cristina Bosco. 2002. Treebank Development: the TUT Approach. In Rajeev Sangal and Sushma M. Bendre (eds.), *Recent Advances in Natural Language Processing. Proceedings of International Conference on Natural Language*

Processing (ICON 2002), Vikas Publ. House, New Delhi, 61-70.

Beth Levin. 1993. *English verb classes and alternations: a preliminary investigation*, University of Chicago Press, Chicago.

Dekang Lin. 1995. A dependency-based method for evaluating broadcoverage parsers. In *Proceedings of the IJCAI-95*, Montreal, Canada, 1420-1425.

Igor Mel'čuk. 1988. *Dependency Syntax: Theory and Practice*, State University Press of New York, Albany/NY.

Cedric Messiant, Anna Korhonen and Thierry Poibeau. 2008. LexSchem: A Large Subcategorization Lexicon for French Verbs. In *Proceedings of the Sixth International Conference on Language Resources and Evaluation (LREC 2008). May 28-30, 2008, Marrakech, Morocco*, European Language Resources Association (ELRA), 2008.

Jarmila Panevová. 1974-1975. *On Verbal Frames in Functional Generative Description*. Part I, «Prague Bulletin of Mathematical Linguistics», 22, 3-40; Part II, «Prague Bulletin of Mathematical Linguistics», 23, 17-52.

Marco Passarotti. 2007. Verso il Lessico Tomistico Biculturale. La treebank dell'*Index Thomisticus*. In Raffaella Petrilli and Diego Femia (eds.), *Il filo del discorso. Intrecci testuali, articolazioni linguistiche, composizioni logiche. Atti del XIII Congresso Nazionale della Società di Filosofia del Linguaggio, Viterbo, 14-16 Settembre 2006*, Aracne Editrice, Pubblicazioni della Società di Filosofia del Linguaggio, 04, Roma, 187-205.

Marco Passarotti. Forthcoming. Theory and Practice of Corpus Annotation in the *Index Thomisticus* Treebank. In *Proceedings of the Conference 'Trends in Computational and Formal Philology - Venice Padua, May 22-24, 2008'*.

Josef Ruppenhofer, Michael Ellsworth, Miriam R.L. Petruck, Christopher R. Johnson and Jan Scheffczyk. 2006. *FrameNet II. Extendend Theory and Practice*. E-book available at http://framenet.icsi.berkeley.edu/index.php?option=com_wrapper&Itemid=126.

Petr Sgall, Eva Hajičová and Jarmila Panevová. 1986. *The Meaning of the Sentence in its Semantic and Pragmatic Aspects*, D. Reidel, Dordrecht, NL.

Lucien Tesnière. 1959. *Éléments de syntaxe structurale*, Editions Klincksieck, Paris, France.

Thomas Aquinas. 1856-1858. *Sancti Thomae Aquinatis, doctoris angelici, Ordinis praedicatorum Commentum in quatuor libros Sententiarum magistri Petri Lombardi, adjectis brevibus adnotationibus*, Fiaccadori, Parma.

Zdenka Urešová. 2004. The Verbal Valency in the Prague Dependency Treebank from the Annotator's Point of View. Jazykovedný ústav Ľ. Štúra, SAV, Bratislava, Slovakia.

Leonoor Van der Beek, Gosse Bouma, Rob Malouf and Gertjan van Noord. 2002. The Alpino Dependency Treebank. In Mariet Theune, Anton Nijholt and Hendri Hondorp (eds.), *Proceedings of the Twelfth Meeting of Computational Linguistics in the Netherlands (CLIN 2001)*, Rodopi, Amsterdam, 8-22.

Applying NLP Technologies to the Collection and Enrichment of Language Data on the Web to Aid Linguistic Research

Fei Xia
University of Washington
Seattle, WA 98195, USA
fxia@u.washington.edu

William D. Lewis
Microsoft Research
Redmond, WA 98052, USA
wilewis@microsoft.com

Abstract

The field of linguistics has always been reliant on language data, since that is its principal object of study. One of the major obstacles that linguists encounter is finding data relevant to their research. In this paper, we propose a three-stage approach to help linguists find relevant data. First, language data embedded in existing linguistic scholarly discourse is collected and stored in a database. Second, the language data is automatically analyzed and enriched, and language profiles are created from the enriched data. Third, a search facility is provided to allow linguists to search the original data, the enriched data, and the language profiles in a variety of ways. This work demonstrates the benefits of using natural language processing technology to create resources and tools for linguistic research, allowing linguists to have easy access not only to language data embedded in existing linguistic papers, but also to automatically generated language profiles for hundreds of languages.

1 Introduction

Linguistics is the scientific study of language, and the object of study is language, in particular *language data*. One of the major obstacles that linguists encounter is finding data relevant to their research. While the strategy of word of mouth or consulting resources in a library may work for small amounts of data, it does not scale well. Validating or reputing key components of a linguistic theory realistically requires analyzing data across a large sample of languages. For instance, in linguistic typology a well-known implicational universal states that if the demonstrative follows the noun, then the relative clause also follows the noun (Croft, 2003). Although this particular universal is well-researched and widely accepted, identifying this tendency anew—as an example of what one must do when researching a new universal—would require a significant amount of work: in order to be relatively sure that the universal holds, the linguist would need to identify a substantial number of true positives (those that support the universal), and ensure that there are not a sufficient number of negatives that would act as a refutation. The only way a linguist could be completely sure would be to conduct a thorough literature review on the subject or go through data from a representative and significant sample of data from the approximately seven thousand languages that are or have been spoken (and for which data exists).

There have been much effort by the linguistic community to address the issue. For instance, LinguistList compiles a long list of linguistic resources[1], making it easier to find electronically available resources. Likewise, the Open Language Archives Community (OLAC) acts as an online virtual library of language resources, and provides a search tool that searches several dozen online linguistic resources. Further, the World Atlas of Language Structures (WALS), which was recently made available online, is a large database of structural (phonological, grammatical, lexical) properties of languages gathered from descriptive materials (Haspelmath et al., 2005).[2]

[1] http://www.linguistlist.org/langres/index.html

[2] There are other online resources for searching for linguistic data, in particular typological data. Two of note include Autotyp (Bickel and Nichols, 2002) and the Typological Database System (Dimitriadis et al., forthcoming), among others. The former has limited online availability (much of

Proceedings of the EACL 2009 Workshop on Language Technology and Resources for Cultural Heritage, Social Sciences, Humanities, and Education –LaTeCH – SHELT&R 2009, pages 51–59,
Athens, Greece, 30 March 2009.

We propose a three-stage approach to help linguists in locating relevant data. First, language data embedded in existing linguistic scholarly discourse is collected and stored in a database. Second, the language data is automatically analyzed and enriched and language profiles are created from the enriched data. Third, a search facility is provided to allow linguists to search the original data, the enriched data, and the language profiles.

This is an on-going research project. While the first stage is completed, the second and third stages are partially completed and still undergoing development. In this paper, we will describe each stage and report results.

2 Related work

In this section, we briefly discuss a few projects that are most relevant to our work.

2.1 Ethnologue

The purpose of the Ethnologue is to provide a comprehensive listing of the known living languages of the world. The most recent version, version 15, covers more than six thousand languages. Information in the Ethnologue comes from numerous sources and is confirmed by consulting both reliable published sources and a network of field correspondents, and has been built to be consistent with ISO standard 639-3; the information is compiled under several specific categories (e.g., countries where a language is spoken and their populations) and no effort is made to gather data beyond those categories (Gordon, 2005).

2.2 WALS

The World Atlas of Language Structures (WALS) is a large database of structural (phonological, grammatical, lexical) properties of languages gathered from descriptive materials (such as reference grammars) by a team of more than 40 linguists (Haspelmath et al., 2005). WALS consists of 141 maps with accompanying text on diverse features (such as vowel inventory size, noun-genitive order, passive constructions, and *hand/arm* polysemy). Each map corresponds to a feature and the map shows the feature values for between 120 and 1370 languages. Altogether there are 2,650 languages and more than 58,000 data points; each data point is a (language, feature, feature value) tuple that specifies the value of the feature in a particular language. For instance, *(English, canonical word order, SVO)* means that the canonical word order of English is SVO.

the data is not directly accessible through query, but requires submitting requests to the site owners), however, and the latter is still under development.

2.3 OLAC

The Open Languages Archive Community (OLAC), described in (Bird and Simons, 2003), is part of the Open Archives Initiative, which promotes interoperability standards for linguistic data.[3] The focus of OLAC has been to facilitate the discovery of linguistic resources through a common metadata structure for describing digital data and by providing a common means for locating these data through search interfaces housed at Linguist List and the Linguistics Data Consortium (LDC). Our work shares with OLAC the need for resource discovery, and moves beyond OLAC by enriching and manipulating the content of linguistic resources.

3 Building ODIN

The first stage of the three-stage approach is to collect linguistic data and store it in a database. In linguistics, the practice of presenting language data in interlinear form has a long history, going back at least to the time of the structuralists. Interlinear Glossed Text, or *IGT*, is often used to present data and analysis on a language that the reader may not know much about, and is frequently included in scholarly linguistic documents. The canonical form of an IGT consists of three lines: a *language line* for the language in question, a *gloss line* that contains a word-by-word or morpheme-by-morpheme gloss, and a *translation line*, usually in English. The grammatical markers such as *3sg* on the gloss line are called *grams*. Table 1 shows the beginning of a linguistic document (Baker and Stewart, 1996) which contains two IGTs: one in lines 30-32, and the other in lines 34-36. The line numbers are added for the sake of convenience.

ODIN, the Online Database of INterlinear text, is a resource built from data harvested from scholarly documents (Lewis, 2006). ODIN was built in three main steps:

(1) Crawling: crawling the Web to retrieve documents that may contain IGTs

[3]http://www.language-archives.org/

1: THE ADJ/VERB DISTINCTION: **EDO** EVIDENCE
2:
3: Mark C. Baker and Osamuyimen Thompson Stewart
4: McGill University
....
27: The following shows a similar minimal pair from **Edo**,
28: a **Kwa** language spoken in Nigeria (Agheyisi 1990).
29:
30: (2) a. *Èmèrí mòsé.*
31: Mary be.beautiful(V)
32: 'Mary is beautiful.'
33:
34: b. *Èmèrí *(yé) mòsé.*
35: Mary be.beautiful(A)
36: 'Mary is beautiful (A).'
...

Table 1: A linguistic document that contains IGT: words in boldface are language names

(2) IGT detection: extracting IGTs from the retrieved documents

(3) Language ID: identifying the language code of the extracted IGTs.

The identified IGTs are then extracted and stored in a database (the ODIN database), which can be easily searched with a GUI interface.[4] In this section, we briefly describe the procedure, and more detail about the procedure can be found in (Xia and Lewis, 2008) and (Xia et al., 2009).

3.1 Crawling

In the first step, linguistic documents that may contain instances of IGT are harvested from the Web using metacrawls. Metacrawling involves throwing queries against an existing search engine, such as Google and Live Search, and crawling only the pages returned by those queries. We found that the most successful queries were those that used strings contained within IGT itself (e.g. grams such as 3sg). In addition, we found precision increased when we included two or more search terms per query, with the most successful queries being those which combined grams and language names.

Other queries we have developed include: queries by language names and language codes (drawn from the Ethnologue database (Gordon, 2005), which contains about 40,000 language names and their variants), by linguists names and the languages they work on (drawn from the Linguist Lists linguist database), by linguistically relevant terms (drawn from the SIL linguistic glossary), and by particular words or morphemes found in IGT and their grammatical markup.

3.2 IGT detection

The canonical form of IGT consists of three parts and each part is on a single line. However, many IGT instances, 53.6% of instances in ODIN, do not follow the canonical form for various reasons. For instance, some IGTs are missing gloss or translation lines as they can be recovered from context (e.g., other neighboring examples or the text surrounding the instance); some IGTs have multiple translations or language lines (e.g., one part in the native script, and another in a latin transliteration); still others contain additional lines of annotation and analysis, such as phonological alternations, underlying forms, etc.

We treat IGT detection as a sequence labeling problem. First, we train a learner and use it to label each line in a document with a tag in a pre-defined tagset. The tagset is an extension of the standard BIO tagging scheme and it has five tags: they are *BL* (any blank line), *O* (outside IGT that is not a BL), *B* (the first line in an IGT), *E* (the last line in an IGT), and *I* (inside an IGT that is not a B, E, or BL). After the lines in a document are tagged by the learner, we identify IGT instances by finding all the spans in the document that match the "B [I | BL]* E" pattern; that is, the span starts with a B line, ends with an E line, and has zero or more I or BL lines in between.

To test the system, we manually annotated 51 documents to mark the positions of the IGTs. We trained the system on 41 documents (with 1573 IGT instances) and tested it on 10 documents (with 447 instances). The F-score for exact match (i.e., two spans match iff they are identical) was 88.4%, and for partial match (i.e., two spans match iff they overlap), was 95.4%. The detail of the system can be found in (Xia and Lewis, 2008).

3.3 Language ID

The language ID task here is very different from a typical language ID task. For instance, the number of languages in ODIN is more than a thousand and could potentially reach several thousand as more data is added. Furthermore, for most languages in ODIN, our training data contains few to no instances of IGT. Because of these properties, applying existing language ID algorithms to the task does not produce satisfactory results. For

[4]http://odin.linguistlist.org

instance, Cavnar and Trenkle's N-gram-based algorithm produced an accuracy of as high as 99.8% when tested on newsgroup articles in eight languages (Cavnar and Trenkle, 1994). However, when we ran the same algorithm on the IGT data, the accuracy fell as low as 2% when the training set was very small.

Since IGTs are part of a document, there are often various cues in the document (e.g., language names) that can help predict the language ID of these instances. We treat the language ID task as a coreference resolution (*CoRef*) problem: a mention is an IGT or a language name appearing in a document, an entity is a language code, and finding the language code for an IGT is the same as linking a mention (e.g., an IGT) to an entity (i.e., a language code).[5] Once the language ID task is framed as a *CoRef* problem, all the existing algorithms on *CoRef* can be applied to the task.

We built two systems: one uses a maximum entropy classifier with beam search, which for each (IGT, language code) pair determines whether the IGT should be linked to the language code; the other treats the task as a joint inference task and performs the inference by using Markov Logic Network (Richardson and Domingos, 2006). Both systems outperform existing, general-purpose language identification algorithms significantly. The detail of the algorithm and experimental results is described in (Xia et al., 2009).

3.4 The current ODIN database

We ran the IGT detection and language ID systems on three thousand IGT-bearing documents crawled from the Web and the extracted IGTs were stored in the ODIN database. Table 2 shows the language distribution of the IGT instances in the database according to the output of the language ID system. For instance, the third row says that 122 languages each have 100 to 999 IGT instances, and the 40,260 instances in this bin account for 21.27% of all instances in the ODIN database.[6]

In addition to the IGTs that are already in the ODIN database, there are more than 130,000 additional IGT-bearing documents that have been crawled but have not been fully processed. Once these additional documents have been processed, the database is expected to expand significantly, growing to a million or more IGT instances.

Table 2: Language distribution of the IGTs in ODIN

Range of IGT instances	# of languages	# of IGT instances	% of IGT instances
> 10000	3	36,691	19.39
1000-9999	37	97,158	51.34
100-999	122	40,260	21.27
10-99	326	12,822	6.78
1-9	838	2,313	1.22
total	1326	189,244	100

4 Analyzing IGT data and creating language profiles

The second stage of the three-stage approach is to analyze and enrich IGT data automatically, to extract information from the enriched data, and to create so-called *language profiles* for the many languages in the database. A *language profile* describes the main attributes of a language, such as its word order, case markers, tense/aspect, number/person, major syntactic phenomena (e.g., scrambling, clitic climbing), etc.[7]

An example profile is shown below. The profile says that in Yoruba the canonical word order is SVO, determiners appear after nouns, and the language has Accusative case, Genitive case, Nominative case, and so on. The concepts such as AccusativeCase come from the GOLD Ontology (Farrar, 2003; Farrar and Langendoen, 2003).

```
<Profile>
  <language code="WBP">Yoruba</language>
  <ontologyNamespace prefix="gold">
     http://linguistic-ontology.org/gold.owl#
  </ontologyNamespace>
  <feature="word_order"><value>SVO</value></feature>
  <feature="det_order"><value>NN-DT</value></feature>
  <feature="case">
     <value>gold:AccusativeCase</value>
     <value>gold:GenitiveCase</value>
     <value>gold:NominativeCase</value>
                    . . .
</Profile>
```

Given a set of IGT examples for a language, the procedure for building a profile for the language has several steps:

(1) Identifying and separating out various fields

[5]A language code is a 3-letter code that *uniquely* identifies a language. In contrast, the mapping between language name and a language is not always one-to-one: some languages have multiple names, and some language names map to multiple languages.

[6]Some IGTs are marked by the authors as ungrammatical (usually with an asterisk "*" at the beginning of the language line). These IGTs are kept in ODIN because they may contain information useful to linguists (for the same reason that they were included in the original linguistic documents).

[7]A thorough discussion on the definition and content of language profiles is beyond the scope of the paper. The reader is referred to (Farrar and Lewis, 2006) for more discussion on the topic.

(language data, gloss, translation, citation, construction name, etc.) in an IGT.

(2) Enriching IGT by processing the translation line and projecting the information onto the language line.

(3) Identifying grams in the gloss line and mapping them to the concepts defined in GOLD Ontology or the like.

(4) Answering questions in the language profile.

In this section, we explain each step and report some preliminary results.

4.1 Identifying fields in IGT

In addition to the language data (*L*), gloss (*G*), and translation (*T*) parts of IGT, an IGT often contains other information such as language name (*-LN*), citation (*-AC*), construction names (*-CN*), and so on. An example is in (1), in which the first line contains the language name and citation,[8] the third line includes coindexes *i* and *i/j*, and the last two lines show two possible translations of the sentence. Here, the language line is displayed as two lines due to errors made by the off-the-shelf converter that converted the crawled pdf documents into text.

```
(1) Haitian CF (Lefebvre 1998:165)
                 ak
    Jani   pale         lii/j
    John   speak  with    he
    (a) 'John speaks with him' (b) 'John
        speaks with himself'
```

The goal of this step is to separate out different fields in an IGT, fix display errors caused by the pdf-to-text converter, and store the results in a uniform data structure such as the one in Ex (2) for the example in Ex (1). The task is not trivial partially because the IGT detector marks only the span of an instance. For instance, the coindex *i* in *Jani* and *lii/j* on the third line of Ex (1) could easily be mistaken as being part of the word.

```
(2) Language: Haitian CF
    Citation: (Lefebvre 1998:165)
    L:         Jan   pale   ak     li
    Coindx:    (Jan, i), (li, i/j)
    G:         John  speak  with   he
    T1:        'John speaks with   him'
    T2:        'John speaks with himself'
```

There has been much work on extracting database records from text or semi-structured sources, and the common approach is breaking the text into multiple segments and labeling each segment with a field name (e.g., (Wellner et al., 2004; Grenager et al., 2005; Poon and Domingos, 2007)). Our task here is slightly different from their tasks (e.g., extracting author/title/journal from citations) in that the fields in IGT could overlap[9] and corrupted lines need to be re-constructed and re-stored in a particular way (e.g., pasting the second and third lines in Ex (1) back together).

Due to the differences, we did not create annotated data by segmenting IGT into separate fields and labeling each field. Instead, we used a refined tagset to indicate what information is available at each line of IGT instances. The tagset includes six main tags (*L*, *G*, *T*, etc.) and nine secondary tags (e.g., *-CR* for corruption and *-SY* for syntactic information). Each line in each IGT instance is labeled with one main tag and zero or more secondary tags. The labeled lines in Ex (1) are shown in (3).

```
(3) M-LN-AC:  Haitian CF (Lefebvre 1998:165)
    L-CR:                     ak
    L-SY-CR:  Jani   pale           lii/j
    G:        John   speak  with    he
    T-DB:     (a) 'John speaks with him' (b) 'John
    C:         speaks with himself'
```

The labeling of the data is done semi-automatically. We have created a tool that takes the IGT spans produced by the current IGT detector and labels IGT lines by using various cues in an IGT instance, and designed a GUI that allows annotators to correct the system output easily. The annotation speed is about 320 IGT instances per hour on average. We are currently experimenting with different ways of re-training the IGT detector with the new data.

We have built a rule-based module that identifies fields in IGT using the enriched tagset (i.e., creating Ex (2) from Ex (3)), relying on the knowledge about the conventions that linguists tend to follow when specifying citations, construction names, coindexation and the like. The initial result of field extraction looks promising. We are also studying whether existing unsupervised statistical systems for information extraction (e.g., (Poon and Domingos, 2007)) could be extended to handle this task while taking advantage of the enriched tagset for IGTs. We plan to complete the study and report the results in the near future.

4.2 Enriching IGT

Since the language line in IGT data typically does not come with annotations (e.g., POS tags, phrase

[8] *CF* here stands for French-lexified creole.

[9] For instance, in some IGTs, a syntactic structure is added on top of the language line; for instance, the language line in Ex (1) could become something like *[IP Jani [VP pale [PP ak lii/j]]]*

structures), we developed a method to enrich IGT data and then extract syntactic information (e.g., context-free rules) to bootstrap NLP tools such as POS taggers and parsers. The enrichment algorithm first parses the English translation with an English parser, then aligns the language line and the English translation via the gloss line, and finally projects syntactic information (e.g., POS tags and phrase structures) from English to the language line. For instance, given the IGT example in Ex (4), the enrichment algorithm would produce the word alignment in Figure 1 and the phrase structures in Figure 2. The algorithm was tested on 538 IGTs from seven languages and the word alignment accuracy was 94.1% and projection accuracy (i.e., the percentage of correct links in the projected dependency structures) was 81.5%. Details of the algorithm and the experiments are discussed in (Xia and Lewis, 2007).

```
(4) Rhoddodd yr  athro   lyfr i'r    bachgen ddoe
    gave-3sg the teacher book to-the boy     yesterday
    ''The teacher gave a book to the boy yesterday''
    (Bailyn, 2001)
```

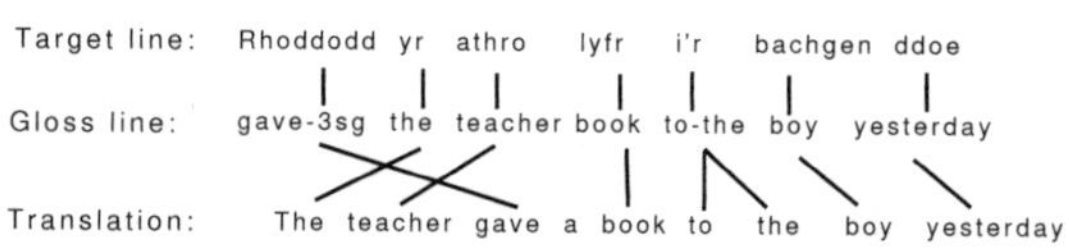

Figure 1: Aligning the language line and the English translation with the help of the gloss line

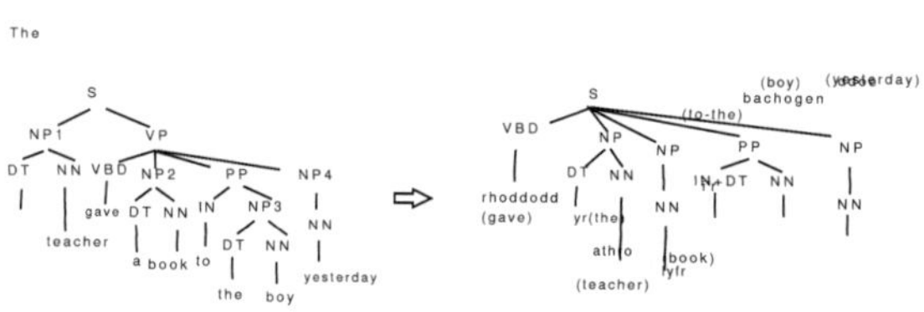

Figure 2: Projecting phrase structure from the translation line to the language line

4.3 Identifying and mapping grams

The third step of Stage 2 identifies grams on the gloss line of an IGT and mapping them to some common semantic so that they can reliably be searched. The gloss line of IGT has two types of glosses: those representing grammatical information (*grams*) such as *NOM*, *3sg*, *PERF*, and standard glosses such as *book* or *give*. Early work in ODIN involved significant manual effort to map grams to GOLD concepts.[10]

The base of several hundred manually mapped grams has provided a reasonably reliable "semantic search" facility in ODIN, which allows linguists to find instances with particular kinds of markup. For example, searching for Perfective Aspect finds instances of data where the data was marked up with PERF, PFV, etc., but also excludes instances that map to "Perfect Tense". While the manually created mapping table covers many common grams, it is far from complete, especially since linguists can coin new grams all the time. We are currently automating the mapping by using the grams in the table as labeled data or seeds and classifying new grams using supervised or semi-supervised methods. This work, however, is still too preliminary to be included in this paper.

4.4 Answering questions in language profiles

The final step of Stage 2 is answering questions in language profiles. Some questions are easier to answer than others. For instance, to determine what grammatical or lexical cases are available in a language according to the data in ODIN, we simply need to look at the grams in the data that map to the case category in GOLD. Other questions are more complex; for instance, to determine whether multiple wh-questions are allowed in a language, we need to examine the projected syntactic structure for the language line and look for the positions of any wh-words that were projected relative to one another. A case study is reported next.

4.5 A case study: Answering typological questions

Two biases are prevalent in IGT data, due to the opportunistic way in which it is harvested and enriched: The first is what we call the *IGT-bias*, that is, the bias produced by the fact that IGT examples are used by authors to illustrate a particular fact about a language, causing the collection of IGT for the language to suffer from a potential lack of representativeness. The second we call the *English-bias*, an English-centrism resulting from the fact that most IGT examples provide an English translation which is used to enrich the language line: as discussed in Section 4.2, the enrichment algorithm assigns a parse tree to the English translation which is then projected onto the langauge line. Since the original parse is built over English data, the projected parse suffers from a bias caused by

[10] See (Lewis, 2006) for more background on mapping grams to GOLD concepts, and (Farrar, 2003) and (Farrar and Langendoen, 2003) for more detailed background on GOLD.

the English source. Because of these biases and errors introduced at various stages of processing, automatically generated language profiles and associated examples should be treated as preliminary and unattested, subject to verification by the linguist. The question is how reliable the profiles are.

To answer the question, we ran a case study in which we evaluated the accuracy of our system in answering a number of typological questions, such as the canonical order of constituents (e.g., sentential word order, order of constituents in noun phrases) or the existence of particular constituents in a language (e.g., determiners). The list of questions and their possible answers are shown in Table 3 (the *WALS #* is a reference number used in WALS (Haspelmath et al., 2005) which uniquely identifies each typological parameter).

In one experiment, we automatically found the answer to the canonical word order question by looking at the context free rules extracted from enriched IGT data. When tested on about 100 languages, the accuracy was 99% for all the languages with at least 40 IGT instances.[12] Not surprisingly, the accuracy decreased for languages with fewer instances (e.g., 65% for languages with 5-9 IGTs). In another experiment, our system answered all the 13 typological questions in Table 3 for 10 languages and the accuracy was 83.1% on average across the questions.

This study shows that, despite potential biases and errors, we can automatically discover certain kinds of linguistic knowledge from IGT with reasonable accuracy and the accuracy increases as more data becomes available. The language profiles built this way could serve as a complement to manually crafted resources such as WALS.

4.6 Comparison with WALS

The task is similar to the goal of the WALS project. In fact, the morphological and syntactic features in WALS form the initial attribute set for our language profiles.[13] The main difference between WALS and our approach is that the information in WALS (including features, feature values, and data points) was gathered by a team of more than 40 linguists, many of them the leading authorities in the field. In contrast, the language profiles in our work are created automatically from opportunistically harvested and enriched linguistic data found on the Web (essentially the IGT in ODIN). Another difference is that our language profiles also include highly language-specific information (e.g., lists of language-specific syntactic constructions, such as *bei-* and *ba-* constructions in Mandarin), as discussed in harvested documents. The information is gathered by checking the construction names included in and surrounding IGT.

The benefits of our approach are twofold. First, we can build language profiles for hundreds of languages with little human effort and the language profiles can be updated whenever the ODIN database is expanded or enriched. Second, each entry in the language profile in ODIN is linked to the relevant IGT instances that are used to answer the question. For instance, a language profile not only lists the canonical word order of the language but also IGT instances from which this information is derived.

5 Extending the search facility

The last stage of the three-stage approach is to provide a search facility for linguists to search the original IGTs, the enriched IGTs and the automatically created language files. The current search interface for ODIN allows a variety of search options, including search by language name or code, language family, and by grams and their related concepts (e.g., Accusative case). Once data is discovered that fits a particular pattern that a user is interested in, he/she can either display the data (where sufficient citation information exists and where the data is not corrupted by the text-to-pdf conversion process) or locate documents from which the data is extracted. Additional search facilities allow users to search across linguistically salient structures ("constructions") and return results in the form of language data and language profiles.

The ODIN database also contains thousands of tree structures for hundreds of languages, each linked to the English tree structures from which they were derived. This can provide unprecedented options for cross-lingual query across "syntactic structures".[14]

[12]Some IGT instances are not sentences and therefore are not useful for answering this question. Further, those instances marked as ungrammatical (usually with an asterisk "*") are ignored for this and all typological questions.

[13]WALS uses the term *feature* to refer to a property such as canonical word order. Since *feature* in NLP has a very different meaning, in this paper we use the term *attribute* instead to avoid potential confusion.

[14]We fully recognize that the projected structures should be considered highly experimental, due to noise in the pro-

Table 3: Thirteen typological questions tested in the case study (ndo=no dominant order, nr=not relevant)

Label	WALS #	Description	Possible Values
		Word Order	
WOrder	330	Order of Words in a sentence	SVO,SOV,VSO,VOS,OVS, OSV,ndo[11]
V+OBJ	342	Order of the Verb, Object and Oblique Object (e.g., PP)	VXO,VOX,OVX,OXV,XVO,XOV,ndo
DT+N	N/A	Order of Nouns and Determiners (*a, the*)	DT-N, N-DT, ndo, nr
Dem+N	358	Order of Nouns and Demonstrative Determiners	Dem-N, N-Dem, ndo, nr
JJ+N	354	Order of Adjectives and Nouns	JJ-N, N-JJ, ndo
PRP$+N	N/A	Order of possessive pronouns and nouns	PRP$-N, N-PRP$, ndo, nr
Poss+N	350	Order of Possessive NPs and nouns	NP-Poss, NP-Poss, ndo, nr
P+NP	346	Order of Adpositions and Nouns	P-NP, NP-P, ndo
		Morpheme Order	
N+num	138	Order of Nouns and Number Inflections (Sing, Plur)	N-num, num-N, ndo
N+case	210	Order of Nouns and Case Inflections	N-case, case-N, ndo, nr
V+TA	282	Order of Verbs and Tense/Aspect Inflections	V-TA, TA-V, ndo, nr
		Existence Tests	
Def	154	Do definite determiners exist?	Yes, No
Indef	158	Do indefinite determiners exist?	Yes, No

We plan to extend the current query facility in three steps to allow these structure-based queries. The first step is to do a user study and identify the types of queries that linguists would be interested in. We have already consulted with a number of syntacticians and other linguists, and have compiled a list of "constructions" that would be of the most interest, and plan to consult with more linguists to extend this list.[15] Some of the initial construction queries have already been implemented in ODIN as "prototypes" for testing purposes. The second step is to identify tools that would facilitate implementing these queries. One such tool is *tgrep2*,[16] which is widely used to search treebank style phrase structures. Since the tool is robust and widely used and supported, we plan to extend it to handle the rich data structures found in the enriched IGT data. The third step is to write a large set of queries in tgrep2 (or other query languages) that "pre-package" the most desirable queries into a form that can be easily executed as a Web service, and design a Web GUI that provides the most accessibility to these queries.

6 Conclusion

One of the major obstacles that linguists encounter is finding data relevant to their research. In this paper, we outline a three-stage procedure to alleviate the problem. First, language data embedded in existing linguistic scholarly discourse is collected and stored in the ODIN database. Second, the language data is automatically analyzed and enriched, and language profiles are created from the enriched data. Our case study shows that knowledge discovery (for the targeted attributes) works reasonably well with even a small amount of IGT data. Third, a search facility is provided that allows linguists to search the original data, the enriched data, and the language profiles by language name, language family, and construction names.

There are several directions for future research. We will improve and thoroughly evaluate the module that extracts various fields from IGT. We will also build more complete language profiles for a dozen or so languages for which we have sufficient IGT data and linguistic knowledge to adequately evaluate the results. Finally, we are exploring ways of extending the query facility (e.g., using *tgrep2*) to allow sophisticated search on the original and enriched IGT data, and plan to provide a GUI with pre-packaged queries which will be easy for linguists to use.

Acknowledgements This work has been supported, in part, by NSF grants BCS-0748919 and BCS-0720670 and a RRF grant from the University of Washington. We would also like to thank four anonymous reviewers for their valuable comments.

jection algorithms, and the resulting structures still need to be reviewed by the linguist throwing the query. However, our case study demonstrates the reasonably high accuracy of answering typological questions with even very limited supplies of data. This supports their utility in spite of noise and error.

[15]A similar study was discussed in (Soehn et al., 2008).

[16]http://tedlab.mit.edu/~dr/TGrep2/

References

John Frederick Bailyn. 2001. Inversion, Dislocation and Optionality in Russian. In Gerhild Zybatow, editor, *Current Issues in Formal Slavic Linguistics*.

Mark C. Baker and Osamuyimen Thompson Stewart. 1996. Unaccusativity and the adjective/verb distinction: Edo evidence. In *Proceedings of the Fifth Annual Conference on Document Analysis and Information Retrieval (SDAIR)*, Amherst, Mass.

Balthasar Bickel and Johanna Nichols. 2002. Autotypologizing databases and their use in fieldwork. In *Proceedings of the LREC Workshop on Resources and Tools in Field Linguistics*, Las Palmas, Spain, Jun.

Steven Bird and Gary Simons. 2003. Extending dublin core metadata to support the description and discovery of language resources. *Computers and the Humanities*, 17(4):375–388.

William B. Cavnar and John M. Trenkle. 1994. N-gram-based text categorization. In *Proceedings of SDAIR-94, 3rd Annual Symposium on Document Analysis and Information Retrieval*, pages 161–175, Las Vegas, US.

William Croft. 2003. *Typology and Universals*. Cambridge University Press, Cambridge, England.

Alexis Dimitriadis, Menzo Windhouwer, Adam Saulwick, Rob Goedemans, and Tams Br. forthcoming. How to integrate databases without starting a typology war: the typological database system. In Simon Musgrave Martin Everaert and Alexis Dimitriadis, editors, *The Use of Databases in Cross-Linguistic Studies*. Mouton de Gruyter, Berlin.

Scott Farrar and D. Terence Langendoen. 2003. A linguistic ontology for the semantic web. *GLOT International*, 7(3):97–100.

Scott Farrar and William D. Lewis. 2006. The GOLD Community of Practice: An infrastructure for linguistic data on the Web. *Language Resources and Evaluation*. Available at http://faculty.washington.edu/wlewis2/papers/FarLew-06.pdf.

Scott Farrar. 2003. *An ontology for linguistics on the Semantic Web*. Ph.d., University of Arizona, May.

Raymond G. Gordon, editor. 2005. *Ethnologue: Languages of the World*. SIL International, Dallas, 15 edition.

T. Grenager, D. Klein, and D. Manning. 2005. Unsupervised learning of field segmentation models for information extraction. In *In Proc. ACL-05*.

Martin Haspelmath, Matthew Dryer David Gil, and Bernard Comrie, editors. 2005. *World Atlas of Language Structures*. Oxford University Press, Oxford.

William Lewis. 2006. ODIN: A Model for Adapting and Enriching Legacy Infrastructure. In *Proc. of the e-Humanities Workshop, held in cooperation with e-Science 2006: 2nd IEEE International Conference on e-Science and Grid Computing*, Amsterdam.

Hoifung Poon and Pedro Domingos. 2007. Joint inference in information extraction. In *Proceedings of the Twenty-Second National Conference on Artificial Intelligence (AAAI)*, pages 913–918, Vancouver, Canada. AAAI Press.

M. Richardson and P. Domingos. 2006. Markov logic networks. *Machine Learning*, pages 107–136.

Jan-Philipp Soehn, Heike Zinsmeister, and Georg Rehm. 2008. Requirements of a user-friendly, general-purpose corpus query interface. In *Proceedings of the LREC 2008 Workshop Sustainability of Language Resources and Tools for Natural Language Processing*, Marrakech, Morocco, May 31.

B. Wellner, A. McCallum, F. Peng, and M. Hay. 2004. An integrated, conditional model of information extraction and coreference with application to citation matching. In *Proc. of the 20th Conference on Uncertainty in AI (UAI 2004)*.

Fei Xia and William Lewis. 2007. Multilingual structural projection across interlinear text. In *Proc. of the Conference on Human Language Technologies (HLT/NAACL 2007)*, pages 452–459, Rochester, New York.

Fei Xia and William Lewis. 2008. Repurposing Theoretical Linguistic Data for Tool Development and Search. In *Proc. of the Third International Joint Conference on Natural Language Processing (IJCNLP-2008)*, Hyderabad, India.

Fei Xia, William D. Lewis, and Hoifung Poon. 2009. Language ID in the Context of Harvesting Language Data off the Web. In *Proceedings of The 12th Conference of the European Chapter of the Association of Computational Linguistics (EACL 2009)*, Athens, Greece, April.

Instance-driven Discovery of Ontological Relation Labels

Marieke van Erp, Antal van den Bosch, Sander Wubben, Steve Hunt
ILK Research Group
Tilburg centre for Creative Computing
Tilburg University
The Netherlands
{M.G.J.vanErp,Antal.vdnBosch,S.Wubben,S.J.Hunt}@uvt.nl

Abstract

An approach is presented to the automatic discovery of labels of relations between pairs of ontological classes. Using a hyperlinked encyclopaedic resource, we gather evidence for likely predicative labels by searching for sentences that describe relations between terms. The terms are instances of the pair of ontological classes under consideration, drawn from a populated knowledge base. Verbs or verb phrases are automatically extracted, yielding a ranked list of candidate relations. Human judges rate the extracted relations. The extracted relations provide a basis for automatic ontology discovery from a non-relational database. The approach is demonstrated on a database from the natural history domain.

1 Introduction

The rapid growth in the digitisation of data has caused many curators, researchers, and data managers of cultural heritage institutions (libraries, archives, museums) to turn to knowledge management systems. Using these systems typically causes them to think about the ontological structure of their domain, involving the identification of key classes in object data and metadata features, and importantly, their relations. The starting point of this process is often a more classical "flat" database matrix model of size $n \times m$, where n is the number of collection items, and m is a fixed number of database columns, typically denoting object metadata features, as cultural heritage institutions are generally well accustomed to using databases of that type. An ontology can be bootstrapped from such a database by first assuming that the database columns can be mapped onto the domain's ontological classes. The next step is then to determine which classes are related to each other, and by which relation. In this paper we present a method that partially automates this process.

To gather evidence for a relation to exist between two ontological classes, it is not possible to simply look up the classes in text. Rather, classes are realised typically as a multitude of terms or phrases. For example, the natural history class "species" is realised as many different instances of species names in text. The automatic discovery of relations between ontological classes thus requires at least a two-step approach: first, the identification of instances of ontological classes in text and their particular relations, and second, the aggregation of these analyses in order to find evidence for a most likely relation.

It is common in ontology construction to use predicative labels for relations. Although no regulations for label names exist, often a verb or verb phrase head is taken, optionally combined with a prepositional head of the subsequent verb-attached phrase (e. g., "occurs in", or "donated by"). In this study, we make the assumption that good candidate labels are frequent verbs or verb phrases found between instances from a particular pair of classes, and that this may sometimes involve a verb-attached prepositional phrase containing one of the two terms. In this paper we explore this route, and present a case study on the discovery of predicative labels on relations in an ontology for animal specimen collections. The first step, identifying instances of ontological classes, is performed by selecting pairs of instances from a flat $n \times m$ specimen database, in which the instances

Proceedings of the EACL 2009 Workshop on Language Technology and Resources for Cultural Heritage, Social Sciences, Humanities, and Education –LaTeCH – SHELT&R 2009, pages 60–68,

are organised by the database columns, and there is a one-to-one relationship between the database columns and the classes in our ontology.

Any approach that bases itself on text to discover relations, is dependent on the quality of that text. In this study we opt for Wikipedia as a resource from which to extract relations between terms. Although the status of Wikipedia as a dependable resource is debated, in part because of its dynamic nature, there is some evidence that Wikipedia can be as reliable a source as one that is maintained solely by experts (Giles, 2005). Wikipedia is also an attractive resource due to its size (currently nearly 12 million articles in over 250 languages). Additionally, Wikipedia's strongly hyperlinked structure closely resembles a semantic net, with its untyped (but directed) relations between the concepts represented by the article topics. Since the hyperlinks in Wikipedia indicate a relations between two encyclopaedia articles, we aim at discovering the type of relation such a link denotes through the use of syntactic parsing of the text in which the link occurs.

The idea of using Wikipedia for relation extraction is not new (Auer and Lehmann, 2007; Nakayama et al., 2008; Nguyen et al., 2007; Suchanek et al., 2006; Syed et al., 2008). However, most studies so far focus on the structured information already explicit in Wikipedia, such as its infoboxes and categories. The main contributions of our work are that we focus on the information need emerging from a specific domain, and that we test a method of pre-selection of sentences to extract relations from. The selection is based on the assumption that the strongest and most reliable lexical relations are those expressed by hyperlinks in Wikipedia pages that relate an article topic to another page (Kamps and Koolen, 2008). The selection procedure retains only sentences in which the topic of the article, identified by matching words in the article title, links to another Wikipedia article. The benefit of the preselection of sentences is that it reduces the workload for the syntactic parser.

Since the system is intentionally kept lightweight, the extraction of relations from Wikipedia is sufficiently fast, and we observe that the results are sufficient to build a basic ontology from the data. This paper is organised as follows. In Section 2 we review related work. In Section 3 the data used in this work is described, followed by the system in Section 4 and an explanation of how we evaluated the possible relations our system discovered is presented in Section 5. We report on the results of our study in Section 6, and formulate our conclusions and points for further research in Section 7.

2 Related Work

A key property of Wikipedia is that it is for the greater part unstructured. On the one hand, editors are encouraged to supply their articles with categories. These categories can be subsumed by broader categories, thus creating a taxonomy-like structure. On the other hand, editors can link to any other page in Wikipedia, no matter if it is part of the same category, or any category at all. An article can be assigned multiple categories, but the number of hyperlinks provided in an average article typically exceeds the number of categories assigned to it.

The free associative hyperlink structure of Wikipedia is intrinsically different from the hierarchical top down architecture as seen in WordNet, as a hyperlink has a direction, but not a type. A Wikipedia article can contain any number of links, pointing to any other Wikipedia article. Wikipedia guidelines state however that wikilinks (hyperlinks referring to another Wikipedia page) should only be added when relevant to the topic of the article. Due to the fact that most users tend to adhere to guidelines for editing Wikipedia pages and the fact that articles are under constant scrutiny of their viewers, most links in Wikipedia are indeed relevant (Blohm and Cimiano, 2007; Kamps and Koolen, 2008).

The structure and breadth of Wikipedia is a potentially powerful resource for information extraction which has not gone unnoticed in the natural language processing (NLP) community. Preprocessing of Wikipedia content in order to extract non-trivial relations has been addressed in a number of studies. (Syed et al., 2008) for instance utilise the category structure in Wikipedia as an upper ontology to predict concepts common to a set of documents. In (Suchanek et al., 2006) an ontology is constructed by combining entities and relations between these extracted from Wikipedia through Wikipedia's category structure and WordNet. This results in a large "is-a" hierarchy, drawing on the basis of WordNet, while further relation enrichments come from Wikipedia's category structure. (Chernov et al., 2006) also exploit the Wikipedia category structure to which concepts in the articles are linked to extract relations.

(Auer and Lehmann, 2007) take a different approach in that they focus on utilising the structure present in infoboxes. Infoboxes are consistently formatted tables in articles that provide summary information, such as information about area, population and language for countries, and birth dates and places for persons. Although infoboxes provide rich structured information, their templates are not yet standardised, and their use has not permeated throughout the whole of Wikipedia.

Although the category and infobox structures in Wikipedia already provide a larger coverage at the concept or term level than for instance WordNet, they do not express all possibly relevant semantic relations. Especially in specific domains, relations occur that would make the Wikipedia data structure unnecessarily dense if added, thus an approach that exploits more of the linguistic content of Wikipedia is desirable.

Such approaches can be found in (Nakayama et al., 2008) and (Nguyen et al., 2007). In both works full sections of Wikipedia articles are parsed, entities are identified, and the verb between the entities is taken as the relation. They also extract relations that are not backed by a link in Wikipedia, resulting in common-sense factoids such as 'Brescia is a city'. For a domain specific application this approach lacks precision. In our approach, we care more for high precision in finding relations than for recall; hence, we carefully pre-select ontological classes among which relations need to be found, and use these as filters on our search.

The usefulness of the link structure in Wikipedia has been remarked upon by (Völkel et al., 2006). They acknowledge that the link structure in Wikipedia denotes a potentially meaningful relation between two articles, though the relation type is unknown. They propose an extension to the editing software of Wikipedia to enable users to define the type of relation when they add a link in Wikipedia. Potentially this can enrich Wikipedia tremendously, but the work involved would be tremendous as well. We believe some of the type information is already available through the linguistic content of Wikipedia.

3 Data Preparation

3.1 Data

The data used in this work comes from a manually created, non-relational research database of a collection of reptiles and amphibians at a natural history museum. The information contained in the cells describes when a specimen entered the collection, under what circumstances it was collected, its current location, registration number, etc. We argue that the act of retrieving information from this flat database could be enhanced by providing a meta-structure that describes relations between the different database columns. If for instance a relation of the type "is part of" can be defined between the database columns *province* and *country*, then queries for specimens found at a particular location can be expanded accordingly.

Even though the main language of the database is Dutch, we still chose to use the English Wikipedia as the resource for retrieval of relation label candidates. Explicitly choosing the English Wikipedia has as a consequence that the relation labels we are bound to discover will be English phrases. Furthermore, articles in the English Wikipedia on animal taxonomy have a broader coverage and are far more elaborate than those contained in the Dutch Wikipedia. Since these database values use a Latin-based nomenclature, using the wider-coverage English Wikipedia yields a much higher recall than the Dutch Wikipedia. The values of the other columns mainly contain proper names, such as person names and geographic locations and dates, which are often the same; moreover, English and Dutch are closely related languages. Different names exist for different countries in each language, but here the inconsistency of the database aids us, as it in fact contains many database entries partially or fully in English, as well as some in German and Portuguese.

The database contains 16,870 records in 39 columns. In this work we focus on 20 columns; the rest are discarded as they are either extrinsic features not directly pertaining to the object they describe, e.g., a unique database key, or elaborate textual information that would require a separate processing approach. The columns we focus on describe the position of the specimen in the zoological taxonomy (6 columns), the geographical location in which it was found (4 columns), some of its physical properties (3 columns), its collector

Column Name	Value
Taxonomic Class	Reptilia
Taxonomic Order	Crocodylia Amphisbaenia
Taxonomic Genus	Acanthophis Xenobatrachus
Country	Indonesia Suriname
Location	city walls near Lake Mahalona
Collection Date	01.02.1888 02.01.1995
Type	holotype paralectotype
Determinator	A. Dubois M. S. Hoogmoed
Species defined by	(Linnaeus, 1758) (LeSueur, 1827)

Table 1: Example classes from test data

and/or determiner, donator and associated date (4 columns), and other information (3 columns). The values in most columns are short, often consisting of a single word. Table 1 lists some example database values.

3.2 Preprocessing

As the database was created manually, it was necessary to normalise spelling errors, as well as variations on diacritics, names and date formats. The database values were also stripped of all non-alphanumeric characters.

In order to find meaningful relations between two database columns, query pairs are generated by combining two values occurring together in a record. This approach already limits the number of queries applied to Wikipedia, as no relations are attempted to be found between values that would not normally occur together. This approach yields a query pair such as *Reptilia Crocodylia* from the taxonomic class and order columns, but not *Amphibia Crocodylia*. Because not every database field is filled, and some combinations occur more often, this procedure results in 186,141 query pairs.

For this study we use a database snapshot of the English Wikipedia of July 27, 2008. This dump contains about 2.5 million articles, including a vast amount of domain-specific articles that one would typically not find in general encyclopaedias. An index was built of a subset of the link structure present in Wikipedia. The subset of links included in the index is constrained to those links occurring in sentences from each article in which the main topic of the Wikipedia article (as taken from the title name) occurs. For example, from the Wikipedia article on *Anura* the following sentence would be included in the experiments[1]:

The frog is an [[amphibian]] in the order Anura (meaning "tail-less", from Greek an-, without + oura, tail), formerly referred to as Salientia (Latin saltare, to jump)

whereas we would exclude the sentence:

An exception is the [[fire-bellied toad]] (Bombina bombina): while its skin is slightly warty, it prefers a watery habitat.

This approach limits the link paths to only those between pages that are probably semantically strongly connected to each other. In the following section the computation of the link paths indicating semantic relatedness between two Wikipedia pages is explained.

3.3 Computing Semantic Relatedness

Relation discovery between terms (instantiations of different ontological classes) that have a page in Wikipedia is best performed after establishing if a sufficiently strong relation between the two terms under consideration actually exists. To do this, the semantic relatedness of those two terms or concepts needs to be computed first. Semantic relatedness can denote every possible relation between two concepts, unlike semantic similarity, which typically denotes only certain hierarchical relations (like hypernymy and synonymy) and is often computed using hierarchical networks like WordNet (Budanitsky and Hirst, 2006).

A simple and effective way of computing semantic relatedness between two concepts c_1 and c_2 is measuring their distance in a semantic network. This results in a semantic distance metric, which can be inversed to yield a semantic relatedness metric. Computing the path-length between terms c_1 and c_2 can be done using Formula 1 where P is the set of paths connecting c_1 to c_2 and Np is the number of nodes in path p.

[1] The double brackets indicate Wikilinks

$$rel_{path}(c_1, c_2) = argmax_{p \in P} \frac{1}{N_p} \quad (1)$$

We search for shortest paths in a semantic network that is constructed by mapping the concepts in Wikipedia to nodes, and the links between the concepts to edges. This generates a very large network (millions of nodes and tens of millions of edges), but due to the fact that Wikipedia is scale-free (Barabasi and Albert, 1999) (its connectedness degree distribution follows a power-law), paths stay relatively short. By indexing both incoming and outgoing links, a bidirectional breadth-first search can be used to find shortest paths between concepts. This means that the search is divided in two chains: a forward chain from c_1 and a backward chain to c_2. As soon as the two chains are connected, a shortest path is found.

4 Extracting Relations from Wikipedia

Each query pair containing two values from two database columns are sent to the system. The system processes each term pair in four steps. A schematic overview of the system is given in Figure 1.

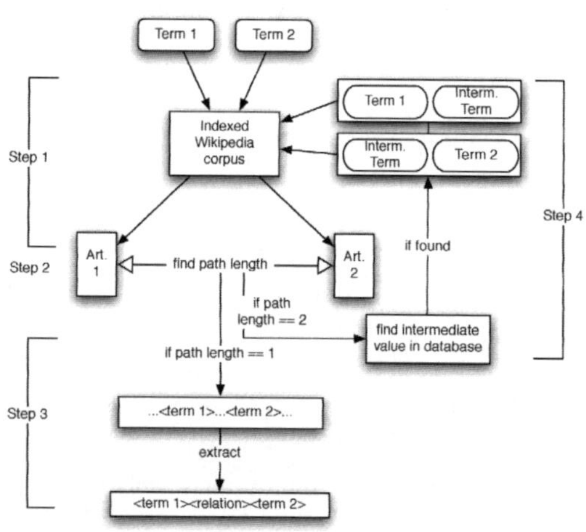

Figure 1: Schematic overview of the system

Step 1 We look for the most relevant Wikipedia page for each term, by looking up the term in titles of Wikipedia articles. As Wikipedia formatting requires the article title to be an informative and concise description of the article's main topic, we assume that querying only for article titles will yield reliable results.

Step 2 The system finds the shortest link path between the two selected Wikipedia articles. If the path distance is 1, this means that the two concepts are linked directly to each other via their Wikipedia articles. This is for instance the case for *Megophrys* from the genus column, and *Anura* from the order column. In the Wikipedia article on *Megophrys*, a link is found to the Wikipedia article on *Anura*. There is no reverse link from *Anura* to *Megophrys*; hierarchical relationships in the zoological taxonomy such as this one are often unidirectional in Wikipedia as to not overcrowd the parent article with links to its children.

Step 3 The sentence containing both target concepts as links is selected from the articles. From the *Megophrys* article this is for instance "*Megophrys is a genus of frogs, order [[Anura]], in the [[Megophryidae]] family*."

Step 4 If the shortest path length between two Wikipedia articles is 2, the two concepts are linked via one intermediate article. In that case the system checks whether the title of the intermediate article occurs as a value in a database column other than the two database columns in focus for the query. If this is indeed the case, the two additional relations between the first term and the intermediate article are also investigated, as well as the second term and that of the intermediate article. Such a bridging relation pair is found for instance for the query pair *Hylidae* from the taxonomic order column, and *Brazil* from the country column. Here, the initial path we find is *Hylidae* $\leftrightarrow$ *Sphaenorhynchys* $\rightarrow$ *Brazil*. We find that the article-in-the-middle value (*Sphaenorhynchys*) indeed occurs in our database, in the taxonomic genus column. We assume this link is evidence for co-occurrence. Thus, the relevant sentences from the Wikipedia articles on *Hylidae* and *Sphaenorhynchys*, and between articles on *Sphaenorhynchys* and *Brazil* are added to the possible relations between "order" – "genus" and "genus" – "country".

Subsequently, the selected sentences are POS-tagged and parsed using the Memory Based Shallow Parser (Daelemans et al., 1999). This parser provides tokenisation, POS-tagging, chunking, and grammatical relations such as subject and direct object between verbs and phrases, and is based on memory-based classification as implemented in TiMBL (Daelemans et al., 2004). The five most frequently recurring phrases that occur between the column pairs, where the subject of the sentence is a value from one of the two columns, are presented to the human annotators. The cut-off of five was chosen to prevent the annotators from having to evaluate too many relations and to only present those that occur more often, and are hence less likely to be misses. Misses can for instance be induced by ambiguous person names that also accidentally match location names (e.g., *Dakota*). In Section 7 we discuss methods to remedy this in future work.

5 Evaluating Relations from Wikipedia

Four human judges evaluated the relations between the ontological class pairs that were extracted from Wikipedia. Evaluating semantic relations automatically is hard, if not impossible, since the same relation can be expressed in many ways, and would require a gold standard of some sort, which for this domain (as well as for many cultural heritage domains) is not available.

The judges were presented with the five highest-ranked candidate labels per column pair, as well a longer snippet of text containing the candidate label, to resolve possible ambiguity. The items in each list were scored according to the total reciprocal rank (TRR) (Radev et al., 2002). For every correct answer $1/n$ points are given, where n denotes the position of the answer in the ranked list. If there is more than 1 correct answer the points will be added up. For example, if in a list of five, two correct answers occur on positions 2 and 4, the TRR would be calculated as $(1/2 + 1/4) = .75$. The TRR scores were normalised for the number of relation candidates that were retrieved, as for some column pairs less than five relation candidates were retrieved.

As an example, for the column pair "Province" and "Genus", the judges were presented with the relations shown in Table 2. The direction arrow in the first column denotes that the "Genus" value occurred before the "Province" value.

The human judges were sufficiently familiar with the domain to evaluate the relations, and had the possibility to gain extra knowledge about the class pairs through access to the full Wikipedia articles from which the relations were extracted. Inter-annotator agreement was measured using Fleiss's Kappa coefficient (Fleiss, 1971).

6 Results and Evaluation

As expected, between certain columns there are more relations than between others. In total 140 relation candidates were retrieved directly, and 303 relation label candidates were retrieved via an intermediate Wikipedia article. We work with the assumption that these columns have a stronger ontological relation than others. For some database columns we could not retrieve any relations, such as the "collection date" field. This is not surprising, as even though Wikipedia contains pages about dates ('what happened on this day'), it is unlikely that it would link to such a domain specific event such as an animal specimen collection. Relations between instances denoting persons and other concepts in our domain are also not discovered through this approach. This is due to the fact that many of the biologists named in the database do not have a Wikipedia page dedicated to them, indicating the boundaries of Wikipedia's domain specific content. Although not ideal, a named-entity recognition filter could be applied to the database after which person names can be retrieved from other resources.

Occasionally we retrieve a Wikipedia article for a value from a person name column, but in most cases this mistakenly matches with a Wikipedia article on a location, as last names in Dutch are often derived from place names. Another problem induced by incorrect data is the incorrect match of Wikipedia pages on certain values from the "Town" and "Province" columns. Incorrect relation candidates are retrieved because for instance the value 'China' occurs in both the "Town" and the "Province" columns. A data cleaning step would solve these two problems.

From each column pair the highest rated relation was selected with which we constructed the ontology displayed in Figure 2. As the figure shows, the relations that are discovered are not only 'is a'-relations one would find in strictly hierarchical resources such as a zoological taxonomy or geographical resource.

The numbers in the relation labels in Figure 2 denote the average TRR scores given by the four judges on all relation label candidates that the judges were presented with for that column pair. The scores for the relations between the taxonomic classes in our domain were particularly high, meaning that in many cases all relation candidates presented to the judges were assessed as

Direction	Label	Snippet
→	is found in	is a genus of venomous pitvipers found in Asia from Pakistan, through India,
→	is endemic to	Cross Frogs) is a genus of microhylid frogs endemic to Southern Philippine,
→	are native to	are native to only two countries: the United States and
→	is known as	is a genus of pond turtles also known as Cooter Turtles, especially in the state of

Table 2: Relation candidates for Province and Genus column pair

correct. The inter-annotator agreement was $\kappa = 0.63$, which is not perfect, but reasonable. Most disagreement is due to vague relation labels such as 'may refer to' as found between "Province" and "Country". If a relation that occurred fewer than 5 times was judged incorrect by the majority of the judges the relation was not included in Figure 2.

Manual fine-tuning and post-processing of the results could filter out synonyms such as those found for relations between "Town" and other classes in the domain. This would for instance define one particular relation label for the relations 'is a town in' and 'is a municipality in' that the system discovered between "Town" and "Province" and "Town" and "Country", respectively.

7 Conclusion and Future Work

In this work we have shown that it is possible to extract ontological relation labels for domain-specific data from Wikipedia. The main contribution that makes our work different from other work on relation extraction from Wikipedia is that the link structure is used as a strong indication of the presence of a meaningful relation. The presence of a link is incorporated in our system by only using sentences from Wikipedia articles that contain links to other Wikipedia articles. Only those sentences are parsed that contain the two terms we aim to find a relation between, after which the verb phrase and possibly the article or preposition following it are selected for evaluation by four human judges.

The advantage of the pre-selection of content that may contain a meaningful relation makes our approach fast, as it is not necessary to parse the whole corpus. By adding the constraint that at least one of the query terms should be the subject of a sentence, and by ranking results by frequency, our system succeeds in extracting correct and informative relations labels. However, there is clearly some room for improvement, for instance in the coverage of more general types of information such as dates and person names. For this we intend to incorporate more domain specific resources, such as research papers from the domain that may mention persons from our database. We are also looking into sending queries to the web, whilst keeping the constraint of hyperlink presence.

Another factor that may help back up the relations already discovered is more evidence for every relation. Currently we only include sentences in our Wikipedia corpus that contain the literal words from the title of the article, to ensure we have content that is actually about the article and not a related topic. This causes many sentences in which the topic is referred to via anaphoric expressions to be missed. (Nguyen et al., 2007) take the most frequently used pronoun in the article as referring to the topic. This still leaves the problem of cases in which a person is first mentioned by his/her full name and subsequently only by last name. Coreference resolution may help to solve this, although accuracies of current systems for encyclopaedic text are often not much higher than baselines such as those adopted by (Nguyen et al., 2007).

Errors in the database lead to some noise in the selection of the correct Wikipedia article. The queries we used are mostly single-word and two-word terms, which makes disambiguation hard. Fortunately, we have access to the class label (i.e., the database column name) which may be added to the query to prevent retrieval of an article about a country when a value from a person name column is queried. We would also like to investigate whether querying terms from a particular database column to Wikipedia can identify inconsistencies in the database and hence perform a database cleanup. Potentially, extraction of relation labels from Wikipedia articles can also be used to assign types to links in Wikipedia.

Acknowledgments

The authors would like to thank the anonymous reviewers for their comments. This research

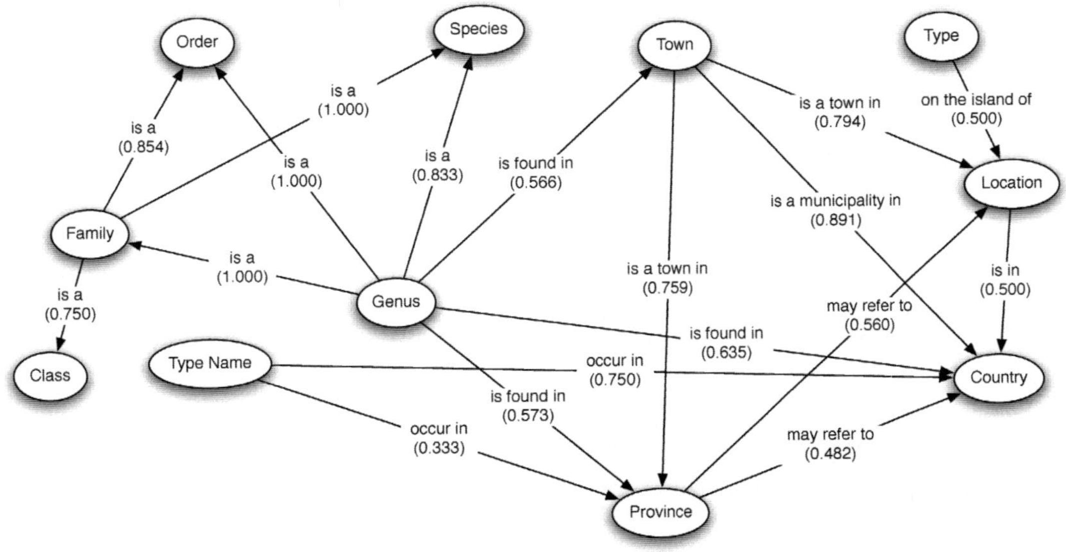

Figure 2: Graph of relations between columns, with TRR scores in parentheses

was funded as part of the Continuous Access to Cultural Heritage (CATCH) programme of the Netherlands Organisation for Scientific Research (NWO).

References

Sören Auer and Jens Lehmann. 2007. What have innsbruck and leipzig in common? extracting semantics from wiki content. In Franconi et al., editor, *Proceedings of European Semantic Web Conference (ESWC'07)*, volume 4519 of *Lecture Notes in Computer Science*, pages 503–517, Innsbruck, Austria, June 3 - 7. Springer.

A. L. Barabasi and R. Albert. 1999. Emergence of scaling in random networks. *Science*, 286(5439):509–512, October.

Sebastian Blohm and Philipp Cimiano. 2007. Using the web to reduce data sparseness in pattern-based information extraction. In *Proceedings of the 11th European Conference on Principles and Practice of Knowledge Discovery in Databases (PKDD)*, Warsaw, Poland, September. Springer.

A. Budanitsky and G. Hirst. 2006. Evaluating WordNet-based measures of lexical semantic relatedness. *Computational Linguistics*, 32(1):13–47.

Sergey Chernov, Tereza Iofciu, Wolfgang Nejdl, and Xuan Zhou. 2006. Extracting semantic relationships between wikipedia categories. In *Proceedings of the First Workshop on Semantic Wikis - From Wiki to Semantics [SemWiki2006] - at ESWC 2006*, pages 153 – 163, Karlsruhe, Germany, May 15.

Walter Daelemans, Sabine Buchholz, and Jorn Veenstra. 1999. Memory-based shallow parsing. In *Proceedings of CoNLL'99*, pages 53–60, Bergen, Norway, June 12.

Walter Daelemans, Jakub Zavrel, Ko Van der Sloot, and Antal Van den Bosch. 2004. Timbl: Tilburg memory based learner, version 5.1, reference guide. Technical Report 04-02, ILK/Tilburg University.

J. L. Fleiss. 1971. Measuring nominal scale agreement among many raters. *Psychological Bulletin*, 76(5):378–382.

Jim Giles. 2005. Internet encyclopaedias go head to head. *Nature*, 438:900–901.

Jaap Kamps and Marijn Koolen. 2008. The importance of link evidence in wikipedia. In Craig Macdonald, Iadh Ounis, Vassilis Plachouras, Ian Rutven, and Ryen W. White, editors, *Advances in Information Retrieval: 30th European Conference on IR Research (ECIR 2008)*, volume 4956 of *Lecture Notes in Computer Science*, pages 270–282, Glasgow, Scotland, March 30 - April 3. Springer Verlag.

Kotaro Nakayama, Takahiro Hara, and Shojiro Nishio. 2008. Wikipedia link structure and text mining for semantic relation extraction towards a huge scale global web ontology. In *Proceedings of SemSearch 2008 CEUR Workshop*, pages 59–73, Tenerife, Spain, June 2.

Dat P. T. Nguyen, Yutaka Matsuo, and Mitsuru Ishizuka. 2007. Exploiting syntactic and semantic information for relation extraction from wikipedia. In *Proceedings of Workshop on Text-Mining & Link-Analysis (TextLink 2007) at IJCAI 2007*, pages 1414–1420, Hyderabad, India, January 7.

Dragomir R. Radev, Hong Q, Harris Wu, and Weiguo Fan. 2002. Evaluating web-based question answering systems. In *Demo section, LREC 2002*, Las Palmas, Spain, June.

F. M. Suchanek, G. Ifrim, and G. Wiekum. 2006. Leila: Learning to extract information by linguistic analysis. In *Proceedings of the ACL-06 Workshop on Ontology Learning and Population*, pages 18–25, Sydney, Australia, July.

Zareen Saba Syed, Tim Finin, and Anupam Joshi. 2008. Wikitology: Using wikipedia as an ontology. Technical report, University of Maryland, Baltimore County.

Max Völkel, Markus Krötzsch, Denny Vrandecic, Heiko Haller, and Rudi Studer. 2006. Semantic wikipedia. In *WWW 2006*, pages 585–594, Edinburgh, Scotland.

The Role of Metadata in the Longevity of Cultural Heritage Resources

Milena Dobreva
Centre for Digital Library Research,
University of Strathclyde
26 Richmond Street Glasgow, G1
1XH, Scotland, United Kingdom
milena.dobreva@strath.ac.uk

Nikola Ikonomov
Institute of Mathematics and
Informatics
bl. 8 Acad. G. Bonchev St.
1113 Sofia, Bulgaria
nikonomov@gmail.com

Abstract

Digital preservation is an integral part of the management of information and the institutions in the cultural heritage sector are seeking for ways to incorporate it into their everyday practice. While there are generic approaches to long-term preservation, further research and development work is needed to address any specifics of the digital objects in the cultural heritage domain. In this paper, we will take two case studies of recent projects and analyse to what extent the metadata accompanying digital objects contribute to guarantee longevity. We summarize this analysis in two scenarios for sustainability of resources produced by small projects because compared to big institutions their digital assets are facing a higher risk not to be preserved properly. We also identify processes where natural language technologies could be of help to make the preservation more efficient.

1 Introduction

An evaluation made in August 2008 in a recent Communication[1] of the EC states that "The absence of clear and comprehensive policies in many Member States was identified in the Recommendation as a threat to the survival of digitised and born-digital material…" It also provides a good practice example from the UK, the Digital Preservation Coalition. Although this British experience is given as an example of a successful approach, the implementation of preservation in the current digital repositories in the UK is far from being satisfactory. The recent final report of the DRAI project (see Daisy Abbott 2008) on UK-based digital repositories identified that "Of the 3,707collections aggregated, only 737 (20%) had evidence of a preservation policy, and of these the vast majority were from within the Arts and Humanities Data Service (AHDS) Collections Repository which, since March 2008, is no longer funded, leaving only 6% of resources with ongoing policies for long term preservation."

Why the digital preservation which is recognised to be of high importance, is still not implemented widely? The Blue Ribbon Task Force Report (2008) summarized five major obstacles in building sustainable digital preservation programs: inadequacy of funding models to address long-term access and preservation needs; confusion and/or lack of alignment between stakeholders, roles, and responsibilities with respect to digital access and preservation; inadequate institutional, enterprise, and/or community incentives to support the collaboration needed to reinforce sustainable economic models; complacency that current practices are good enough; and fear that digital access and preservation is too big to take on. While these address mostly stakeholder-related issues, a recent report (DPE: 2007) reviewed the progress of digital preservation **research** world-wide. It concludes that "The analysis of the last 16 years of effort in the area of digital preservation… support our claim that while much work has been done on the periphery, the central problems of digital preservation

[1] Communication from the Commission to the Council, the European Parliament, the European Economic and Social Committee and the Committee of the Regions *Europe's cultural heritage at the click of a mouse. Progress on the digitisation and online accessibility of cultural material and digital preservation across the EU* [SEC(08) 2372] of 11 August 2008. Available: http://ec.europa.eu/information_society/activities/digital_libraries/doc/communications/progress/communication_en.pdf

Proceedings of the EACL 2009 Workshop on Language Technology and Resources for Cultural Heritage, Social Sciences, Humanities, and Education –LaTeCH – SHELT&R 2009, pages 69–76,
Athens, Greece, 30 March 2009. ©2009 Association for Computational Linguistics

have yet to be resolved." Automation in digital preservation is one of the ten areas named by this study as being in a need of accelerated research.

These two reports identify two key areas which need attention: the organisational aspects and the research. Any institution which currently faces the preservation challenge has to make a difficult choice under the circumstances of the rapidly changing technological environment and the lack of a generally recommended and effective solution.

However, the deeper reason why after two decades of efforts digital preservation still has not reached maturity, is the lack of consistent theoretical foundation. In 2001, James Cheney et al. articulated the need to develop a mathematical theory for the area of information preservation. Having such a theory should help to understand better the object models and the basic transformations which need to be supported in a preservation system; it will also be of great benefit to automation because it would be much more clear what processes can be automated. In addition, a coherent theory would help to identify any gaps in procedures or data flows and thus would contribute to the implementation of systems which behaviour could be consistently traced. However, since this first suggestion that a theory of preservation is needed, there has not been much progress in developing one. Even the identification of the basic elements of a theory of preservation is not a trivial task.

In addition to this methodological difficulty, the variety of domains where digital preservation is to be applied brings even more difficulties. It is still not clear whether a universal 'one-size-fits-all' solution could be used in all different domains. For example, in the cultural heritage domain which is considered in this paper there are various curatorial situations with regard to digital objects. Resources prepared by small projects are in more danger with regard to their longevity compared to resources of large institutions if we consider that they are created but the lifecycle for digital objects curation is not applied in full. In this paper it is not our aim to investigate what is the level of awareness and readiness of the whole range of cultural heritage institutions but we try to highlight what is the current state in the digital preservation field and what issues need to be addressed by projects in the cultural heritage domain.

In 2002, the reference model for an open archival information system (OAIS) was published and one year later adopted in the international standard ISO 14721:2003, see (OAIS: 2003). It provides a functional approach which is helpful to understand and describe the processes in a preservation system. However, the specification of the minimum information which should accompany a digital object in order to guarantee its accessibility, interpretability and usability in the future, is not addressed in OAIS.

There are different ongoing attempts to build a theory of preservation. Giorgos Flouris and Carlo Meghini in 2007 again suggested basing such a theory on firm mathematical foundations and such an effort will be made within the CASPAR[2] project. Paul Watry in 2007 presented the directions of future research of the SHAMAN[3] project which aims to study the context which guarantees that the essential properties of digital objects such as authenticity and integrity will be maintained over time. Reagan Moore and MacKenzie Smith suggested in 2007 a practical approach, which demonstrates how various requirements of the preservation systems can be implemented as sets of rules.

Attempts to find an approach to building a coherent theory of preservation should also reflect the specific features of various subject domains.

In Section 2 of this paper, we introduce the basic concepts of the ISO standard in the digital preservation domain OAIS[4]. Then in Section 3 we discuss issues related to the use of metadata for preservation in the cultural heritage domain. We take two examples of resources under preparation in the TEXTE project[5] and the KT-DigiCult-BG[6] project and suggest two scenarios for preservation of the products of small projects. In Section 4 we summarise the issues which need further development in the cultural heritage sector in order to address better the issue of longevity of the digital resources.

---

[2] CASPAR – Cultural, Artistic and Scientific knowledge for Preservation, Access and Retrieval – an Integrated Project co-financed by the EU within FP6. http://www.casparpreserves.eu/caspar-project

[3] SHAMAN – Sustaining Heritage Access through Multivalent ArchiviNg an Integrated Project co-financed by the EU within FP7. http://shaman-ip.eu/

[4] Open archival information system, see OAIS 2003.

[5] TEXTE: Transfer of Expertise in Technologies of Editing, funded under the Marie Curie programme of FP6, http://www.nuigalway.ie/mooreinstitute/projects.php?project=15

[6] Knowledge Transfer in Digitisation of Cultural and Scientific Heritage to Bulgaria, funded under the Marie Curie programme of FP6, http://www.math.bas.bg/digi/indexen.html

2 The Basic Standard in the Digital Preservation Domain: OAIS

In response to the increased need for the introduction of common practices in assuring long term digital preservation (DP) of digital objects, the International Standards Organisation (ISO) in the last decade developed a number of conceptual DP standards and also some technical guidelines. The most popular standard in the area is ISO 14721:2003 (Space data and information transfer systems – Open archival information system – Reference model), widely known as OAIS[7].

It is a conceptual framework which presents the main functional components and identifies the basic data flows within a digital preservation system. The development of OAIS[8] arose from the need for a model which would specify the basic components of a system for long-term preservation of digital objects and their relationships with the 'external world'.

In Fig. 1, an OAIS is represented as a box which is connected to other entities from the environment. These are **Producers**, **Consumers**, and **Management (**OAIS is not suggesting what roles could be defined within the archive). A special class of Consumers is the **Designated Community**. The Designated Community is the set of Consumers who should be able to understand the preserved information."[9]

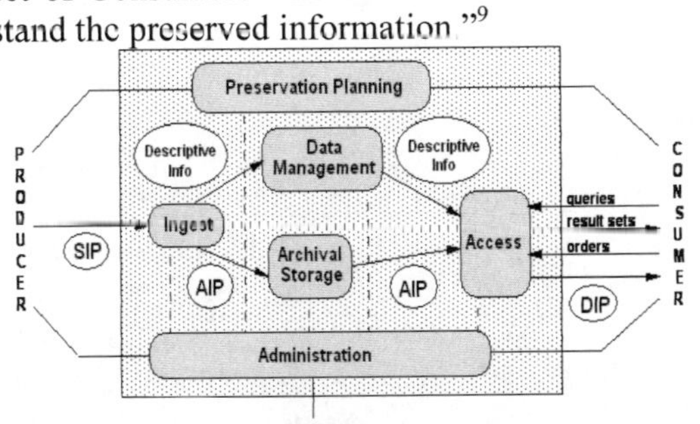

Figure 1: The OAIS functional entities and environment[10]

Within the cultural heritage domain, a special attention also should be paid to the concept of designated community which is essential for the understanding of resources in the future. Understanding the actual needs and the level of background knowledge of the designated community is not trivial in this domain, especially in the cases of creating scholarly resources.

This in fact opens a new essential issue related to the dynamics of resources: while the resources created by memory institutions such as libraries, archives and museums are 'static' because they represent the resources of the institutions, the resources created by projects tend to be dynamic, because they could be enriched and extended. These resources usually do not cover a fixed set of holdings but are oriented towards a specific theme and after a core set of resources is available, more materials could be added at later stages. Being familiar with the model will help cultural heritage professionals to organize better the digital objects' lifecycle and take informed decisions on the preservation aspects of their resources.

In addition to the definition of these functional entities, an OAIS information model explains the data flows between the environment and the archive, and also within the functional components of the archive.

Every act of submission of information to an OAIS by a Producer, as well as the dissemination of information to a Consumer, occurs either as a single discrete transmission, or as a series of transmissions. To describe the exchange of data, OAIS defines the concept of an **Information Package** as a "container" of two types of information: **Content Information (CI)** and **Preservation Description Information (PDI)**. The Content Information and PDI are viewed as being encapsulated and identifiable by the **Packaging Information (PI)**.

OAIS defines three specialised types of information packages (IP), namely:

- Archival Information Package (AIP): An Information Package, consisting of the Content Information and the associated PDI, which is preserved within an OAIS.
- Dissemination Information Package (DIP): The Information Package, derived from one or more AIPs, received by the Consumer in response to a request to the OAIS.
- Submission Information Package (SIP): An Information Package that is delivered by the Producer to the OAIS for use in the construction of one or more AIPs.

PDI is divided into four types of preservation information called *Provenance, Context, Refer-*

[7] A webpage which provides information on the basic stages of its development is http://nost.gsfc.nasa.gov/isoas/.
[8] For a record of the activities see http://nssdc.gsfc.nasa.gov/nost/isoas/.
[9] Source: p.2.2-2.3, OAIS (2003).
[10] Source: Figure 4-1, page 4-1 (OAIS, 2003).

ence, and *Fixity*. Provenance describes the source of the Content Information; Context describes how the CI relates to other information outside the Information Package. Reference provides identifiers, by which the CI may be uniquely identified. Fixity provides a wrapper, which protects the CI from undocumented alteration. A key point to note is that OAIS does not suggest any specific metadata as instantiations of PDI; so that there is no guidance on what constitutes a minimum technical requirement in respect of representing and encoding PDI information within corresponding PDI data bitstreams. The definition of a minimum required set of data should be based on a study of what is required to assure a reliable, consistent, and measurable specification and implementation of a preservation system.

The consequences for the cultural heritage domain is that currently there is no single and uniformly accepted set of elements which guarantee the longevity of resources; but every single institution and project should consider how to structure the different types of archival packages if it establishes and digital archive and also decide what metadata need to be stored for preservation purposes.

In OAIS the closest analogue to the high-level notion of metadata can be found in the idea of *representation information* while on the implementation level PDI provides the closest notion to a particular instantiation of a set of metadata elements.

Having a reference framework for long-term digital preservation systems had an essential impact on the development of a common professional understanding and vocabulary. It has had a significant impact on the subsequent development of standards and as a guide to the setting up of preservation systems. Yet, the complexity of the area allows for multiple interpretations of how the framework should be implemented in real life applications. This arguably gives rise to a need to develop implementation guidelines and also to adjust any practical solution to policy frameworks.

3 Preservation-Related Metadata

3.1 Metadata for Preservation vs. Preservation of Existing Metadata

There are two key issues which need to be considered vis-à-vis metadata and preservation.

1. What metadata are needed for preservation purposes in the cultural heritage domain (besides assuring a reliable preservation process, they should help the designated communities to understand the resources), and
2. How to preserve the metadata accompanying existing digital objects. Since it is often the case that cultural heritage resources have extensive metadata and there are multiple schemes used, this issue also touches upon understanding and use of present metadata schemes in the future; this issue is very similar to interoperability of metadata schemes but considered as interoperability between now and the future.

In the area of preservation metadata, the basic concern, as stated by Brian Lavoie and Richard Gartner, still seems to be the development of preservation elements' schemes (2005). However, presentation and interoperability issues are not the only concern: preservation metadata, as all other types of metadata are affected by the metadata bottleneck[11], a metaphor which indicates that the human efforts needed to create metadata can not cope with the pace of creation of new digital resources.

Another disquieting example comes from a recent evaluation of a German national digitisation programme which reveals "insufficient metadata practice, endangering the usage of the digital documents, not to speak of their preservation: 33% of the objects had no metadata at all, 33% bibliographic metadata only, 10% had both bibliographic and subject metadata (rest: no information). Less than a third of the metadata was digital."[12]

To suggest an OAIS-compliant preservation metadata solution, in 2002 OCLC (Online Computer Library Center, Inc.) and RLG (Research Libraries Group) created a working group to explore how a consensus between different projects and initiatives in the field of preservation metadata could be achieved. A body of recommended metadata for digital preservation was developed in the next years under the name PREMIS: PREservation Metadata Implementation Strategies (see PREMIS (2008)). The effort of OCLC and RLG to define preservation metadata is a major development in the digital preservation field. However, it analyses only preservation metadata related to the digital object itself. A number of issues likely to appear in real imple-

[11] The term metadata bottleneck was coined by E. Liddy in 2002.

[12] DELOS brainstorming on Metadata topics, Juan les Pins, 05/12/2005, http://www.ukoln.ac.uk/ukoln/staff/t.koch/pres/Brainst200512-MDc.html

mentation scenarios are not considered, for example the preservation and re-use of descriptive and other metadata which might have been supplied with the digital object which is of special importance in the cultural heritage domain. Such metadata could be of help in generating preservation metadata, or could be later used for search.

Having all these in mind, preservation metadata area provides many challenges. What preservation metadata to use? What minimum set needs to be supplied in order to guarantee a reliable preservation process? How to automate the creation of preservation metadata? How to guarantee that the digital resources developed within a particular project are accompanied by sufficient preservation quality metadata? And how to guarantee interoperability between multiple existing schemes? It is not easy for any organisation or project to make decisions regarding the metadata in this situation.

In the last years there were several metadata schemes developed dedicated to long-term preservation. In the domain of cultural heritage institutions these new kind of metadata have to be combined with existing descriptive metadata based on the traditionally used catalogue systems. Amongst those we are The Metadata Encoding and Transmission Standard[13] (METS), a container format for metadata and content files maintained by the Library of Congress (USA); and LMER (Long-term preservation Metadata for Electronic Resources)[14] developed by the German National Library.

Currently, researchers come to the conclusion that the practical preservation activities require to combine several various metadata schemes to achieve a reliable preservation process. For example Angela Dappert and Markus Enders (2008) present an example of integrating METS, PREMIS, and MODS[15] metadata in an OAIS-compatible system which aims to ingest, store, and preserve eJournals in the British Library. They demonstrated that no single existing metadata schema accommodates the representation of descriptive, preservation and structural metadata necessary for such a system.

3.2 Two Examples

3.2.1. The TEXTE Project Digital Resources

TEXTE is an ongoing project coordinated by The Moore Institute in the National University of Ireland, Galway. It combines four tasks which aim to illustrate how the current computer-enhanced editing tools can be used to produce various types of high-quality scholarly editions (mediaeval manuscripts; correspondence; a set of journal issues and ephemera). The materials are digitised and then transcribed and encoded using the Guidelines of the Text Encoding Initiative[16]. The resulting resources are highly annotated scholarly editions, a combination of the original texts with the scholarly findings.

All these resources are built using the same guidelines for text encoding. This common framework facilitates the development of the digital objects especially with regard to their online publication and visualisation and to the annotation of resources from the same historical and cultural background.

From digital preservation point of view, there are several issues which need to be taken into account:

The TEI P5: Guidelines for Electronic Text Encoding and Interchange[17] are not suggesting metadata elements to be used especially for preservation purposes. It is essential to have well-formed <TEI.Header> and to document the principles applied in the encoding of the text; these are prepared as a part of the project documentation. But the <TEI.Header> currently does not support elements which can help to trace the digital object's authenticity, integrity and chain of custody – these could be included as additions. But a difficulty for such projects is the lack of guidance on the significant properties of digital objects which need to be supported.

Projects such as TEXTE developing textual resources would benefit from clear guidance on this matter; currently the project faces the need to find its own solution. The final product of TEXT will be a set of web resources but their inclusion into repository is still under question; if this happens additional effort will be needed to define SIPs and to transform currently available XML files into SIPs.

[13] http://www.loc.gov/standards/mets/

[14] LMER description and LMER schema: http://www.d-nb.de/eng/standards/lmer/lmer.htm

[15] http://www.tei-c.org/index.xml

[16] Metadata Object Description Schema, MODS, http://www.loc.gov/standards/mods/

[17] http://www.tei-c.org/release/doc/tei-p5-doc/en/html/index-toc.html

On the other metadata-related issue, the longevity of specific metadata schemes applied in the cultural heritage domain, the decision to use a widespread encoding framework might be seen as a guarantee of the future usability of resources. This is based on the expectation that the TEI will be continuously supported in the future.

3.2.2. The KT-DigiCult-BG Project Digital Resources

The KT-DigiCult-BG project funded by the Marie Curie programme of FP6 was recently finished (in 2008) and one of its outcomes was the creation of the Digitisation Centre in the Institute of Mathematics and Mathematics at the Bulgarian Academy of Sciences (IMI-BAS). This centre digitised a substantial number of various types of objects belonging to the Bulgarian cultural and scientific heritage (see Table 2). One of the issues the project faced was the organisation and the long-term preservation of these objects. These resources were not deeply annotated and are intended for the most general type of users – the citizens. In this case the metadata used in the mix of archival materials, old printed books, photographs and periodicals followed various encodings and were not encoded like the metadata of the TEXTE project using the same Guidelines.

This heterogeneity of approaches leads to a different situation in the produced resources. Currently the digitisation centre team is planning to place all scientific resources into a repository using DSpace[18] which will enable the use of its resources within the DRIVER[19] project repository.

Preservation-wise, these resources will be transformed according to this larger initiative requirements and the relevant SIP will be built. In this scenario the preservation task with regard to the digitised documents prepared for access in PDF format stays with the repository while the digitisation centre will take care for the physical copying of the master files which are stored in TIFF format. This is a mixed approach where various bodies take care for the preservation of clusters of digital resources.

[18] http://www.dspace.org/

[19] DRIVER: Networking European Scientific Repositories, http://www.driver-repository.eu/.

Table 2. Digitised Resources in 2005-08 in IMI-BAS

Type of material	Size
Old printed books (National Library Ivan Vazov, Plovdiv)	17,000 pages
State Archives	8,000 pages
Research Archive of the Academy of Sciences	24 archival units, 1,000 pages
Old periodicals (newspapers)	1,200 pages
Musical periodicals	1,000 pages
Archive of the Higher Attestation Commission	8,500 pages
Archive of IMI-BAS	18,000 pages
Mathematical heritage (the heritage of Prof. Obreshkov)	2,000 pages
Audio archive of Bulgarian dialects	7 hours
Mathematical periodicals (1905 - 1991)	29,000 pages
Old photographs	200 photographs
TOTAL	85,900 units

3.3 Two Emerging Scenarios for Digital Preservation of Small Projects' Outputs

Two scenarios emerge from the analysis of the two case studies.

Scenario 1. Preparation of stand-alone resources. Under this scenario, the set of digital resources is prepared as a stand-alone collection and does not necessarily become a part of a digital repository.

1. Such projects need to pay special attention to proper documentation of the decisions taken on the encoding applied within the project – this is not only substantial for sustainability, but also for re-use of resources in the future as demonstrated by Claire Warwick et al. (2009). Documentation which refers to a general standard like TEI or XML is not sufficient because it does not guarantee future understanding and interoperability.
2. A set of preservation metadata needs to be supplied for every single digital object. This is currently not a trivial requirement because there is no common view on the structure of preservation metadata. Again, the internal project decisions need to be well-documented.
3. The overall responsibility to document significant properties of the digital objects which will allow checking authenticity and chain of custody stays with the project; it is unlikely to expect that anyone in the future will be able to fill in such gaps if they are present.

Scenario 2. Preparation of resources which will be integrated into a larger digital repository. The following key considerations should be taken into account:

1. It is essential to be familiar with the processes of ingest of digital objects into the repository.
2. The structure of the SIPs for ingest should be discussed in advance.
3. The significant properties of digital objects need to be discussed with the digital repository; it should guarantee to retain authenticity and chain of custody related to the ingested objects.

The following Analysis Matrix (see Table 3) summarizes what issues needs to be taken into account in these scenarios.

Table 3. Summary of digital-preservation issues reflected in the two suggested scenarios

Issue	Scenario 1. (stand-alone resources)	Scenario 2. (resources to be integrated into a digital repository)
Digital object	The digital object is prepared completely and solely within the project.	The digital object is likely to be enriched in order to be ingested into a repository. This enrichment can be done by various parties according to the adopted procedures for ingest into the repository.
Significant properties of the digital object	Small projects usually do not consider significant properties but they are essential as future evidence of authenticity, integrity and chain of custody.	The values of the significant properties which guarantee authenticity, integrity and chain of custody need to be supplied jointly with the digital object when it is being ingested into the digital repository.
Preservation actions	The preservation actions e.g. copying of media or migration to newer file formats will be applied within the host institution; it needs to plan for these otherwise the danger is that the collection as a whole (or separate objects) will be lost because of media decay.	The preservation actions are applied within the repository. The creators of the collection do not have to plan for this but need to make sure what are the digital repositories policies on physical copying and format migration.
OAIS implementation	It is unlikely that small projects will implement the complete set of OAIS functional entities.	The repository hosting the project outputs may implement a specific subset of OAIS functional entities; this should be discussed in advance as a sustainability guarantee.
Possible application of natural language processing (NLP) technology	NLP can be applied for automated generation of metadata, including preservation metadata; we do not have evidence of such attempts so far.	An area of active research is the application of NLP for automated extraction of metadata from digital objects during ingest. This will help to overcome the metadata bottleneck.

We hope that this succinct analysis will help projects to understand better the preservation-related options they have.

4 Conclusions

Our presentation of digital preservation issues and the specifics of cultural heritage domain pinpoints several issues which are essential for future implementations:

1. The understanding of digital preservation standards and models is essential to organise a proper lifecycle management for the cultural heritage resources; there are examples of solutions applied in the large memory institutions[20] but smaller projects and initiatives need to address these issues when they develop their sustainability plans.
2. Widely used metadata standards in the cultural heritage domain, such as TEI, could offer better guidance on metadata elements subset designed especially to support long-term preservation. TEI provides mechanisms for follow-

[20] The German National Library and the Royal Library in the Netherlands are examples of institutions which apply successfully digital preservation solutions.

ing any changes in the digital object; it also could be used to encode information related to other copies made such as master or preservation copies and access or use copies; and possibly to record any processes applied to a resource, but this is not sufficient because it reflects the process of creation of an object but this is not sufficient to claim authenticity of this object. Currently there is no mechanism to check the integrity and the chain of custody of digital objects. However, TEI guidelines should suggest how correctly to represent these changes. For example Linda Cantara in 2005 suggested to form an AIP for the resources of the *Tibet Oral History Archive Project* especially for digital preservation purposes; more examples are needed in order to establish a good practices which could be incorporated in other cases.

3. OAIS does not suggest any specific metadata as instantiations of preservation description information and in particular in the cultural heritage domain there is no single and uniformly accepted set of elements which guarantee the longevity of resources; therefore it is necessary to define what metadata need to be stored for preservation purposes. We can not offer a general solution to this problem because it requires consensus of the communities of professionals.

We also have presented two scenarios on digital preservation derived from case studies on two EC-funded projects. This work shows that there is definitely a current need to suggest good practices for such endeavours, because while the projects tackle the preservation issue, it is very difficult to find individual good models to guarantee the longevity of resources.

Reference

Angela Dappert and Markus Enders. 2008. Using METS, PREMIS and MODS for Archiving eJournals. In: *D-Lib Magazine* September/October 2008, Vol. 14, Number 9/10, ISSN 1082-9873 Available: http://www.dlib.org/dlib/september08/dappert/09dappert.html

Blue Ribbon. 2008. The Blue Ribbon Task Force on Sustainable Digital Preservation and Access (2008). Interim Report. Available: http://brtf.sdsc.edu/biblio/BRTF_Interim_Report.pdf

Brian Lavoie and Richard Gartner. 2005. Preservation metadata, DPC Technology Watch Series Report 05-01. Available: http://www.dpconline.org/docs/reports/dpctw05-01.pdf

Claire Warwick, Isabel Galina, Jon Rimmer, Melissa Terras, Ann Blandford, Jeremy Gow, George Buchanan (2009) Documentation and the Users of Digital Resources in the Humanities. Journal of Documentation, Vol. 65 (1), pp. 33-57.

Daisy Abbott. 2008. JISC Final Report – Digital Repositories and Archives Inventory Project, HATII, University of Glasgow, July 2008.

DPE. 2007. Digital Preservation Europe (DPE) (2007). Access to and preservation of cultural and scientific resources: research roadmap. http://www.digitalpreservationeurope.eu/publications/reports/dpe_research_roadmap_D72.pdf

Giorgos Flouris and Carlo Meghini. 2007. Some Preliminary Ideas Towards a Theory of Digital Preservation, 2007, Proceedings of the 1st International Workshop on Digital Libraries Foundations (DLF1-07). Available: http://www.ite.gr/ics/isl/publications/paperlink/DLF107.pdf

James Cheney, Carl Lagoze and Peter Botticelli. 2001. Towards a Theory of Information Preservation . In: Constantopoulos & I.T. Sølvberg (Eds.): ECDL 2001, LNCS 2163: 340–351, Springer-Verlag Berlin Heidelberg.

Linda Cantara. 2005. The *Tibet Oral History Archive Project* and Digital Preservation. ACH-ALLC 2005 conference. Available: http://mustard.tapor.uvic.ca/cocoon/ach_abstracts/xq/xhtml.xq?id=141

OAIS. 2003. ISO 14721:2003 (Space data and information transfer systems – Open archival information system – Reference model). Available: http://public.ccsds.org/publications/archive/650x0b1.pdf

Paul Watry. (2007). Digital Preservation Theory and Application: Transcontinental Persistent Archives Testbed Activity. International Journal of Digital Curation 2(2). Available: http://www.ijdc.net/ijdc/article/view/43/0

PREMIS. (2008) Data Dictionary for Preservation Metadata: PREMIS version 2.0, Available: http://www.loc.gov/standards/premis/v2/premis-2-0.pdf.

Reagan Moore and MacKenzie Smith. (2007). Automated Validation of Trusted Digital Repository Assessment Criteria. Journal of Digital Information 8(2). Available: http://journals.tdl.org/jodi/article/view/198/181.

Association for Computational Linguistics
209 N. Eighth Street
Stroudsburg, Pennsylvania 18360

CURRAN ASSOCIATES INC
proceedings.com